Ken's Gu

KEN'S GUIDE
to the
BIBLE

Ken Smith

BLAST BOOKS
NEW YORK

Ken's Guide to the Bible © 1995 Ken Smith

Blast Books gratefully acknowledges the generous help of
Beth Escott and Don Kennison.

FRONTISPIECE: *The widow Rizpah hangs out with several members of her family.
She is praised in the Bible for her loyalty to the rotting corpses of her sons, using a
stick to fend off hungry carrion birds for weeks on end. Rizpah's innocent boys
were crucified to appease God but, hey, tough luck.* (II SAMUEL 21:1–10)

Published by Blast Books, Inc.
P. O. Box 51, Cooper Station
New York, NY 10276-0051

Designed by Laura Lindgren

ISBN 0-922233-17-9
Manufactured in the United States of America
First Edition 1995
10 9 8 7 6 5 4 3 2 1

For Uzzah the ox-cart driver
who deserved better.

Contents

Acknowledgments

This guide would not exist were it not for the faith, encouragement, and talents of the following:

Susie Kirby shared her scholarship, Doug Kirby his artistic talents, and both generously fortified Yours Truly with their insights and much-appreciated moral support.

A bow of gratitude to Carol Autori, my ray of sunshine in the murky corridors of power.

Many kudos to the staff and resources of the Newark Public Library, main branch, an overlooked gem of an institution.

Thanks also to Toni DeMarco, Don Faller, and Mike Wilkins, for friendship and kindness that Jesus would've glorified; to Anne Bernstein, Dan Lieb, and Fred Malley, for putting me hip to things I otherwise would have missed; and to my family, who still tolerates my eccentricities after all these years.

Research sources for this guide, in addition to the Bible versions listed elsewhere, include *The Westminster Aids to Scripture Study*, *The King James Bible Dictionary*, *Strong's Bible Concordance*, *The Outline of History* by H. G. Wells, The Anchor Bible, The New Jerusalem Bible, and *Asimov's Guide to the Bible*, which was also a source of inspiration and insights.

Introduction

"Will the one who contends with the Almighty correct him?"

—JOB 40:2

". . . who are you, O man, to talk back to God?"

—ROMANS 9:20

"Warn a divisive person once, and then warn him a second time. After that, have nothing to do with him. You may be sure that such a man is warped and sinful; he is self-condemned."

—TITUS 3:10–11

Do people who pray to bleeding statues give you the willies? Do Darwin-bashing school boards and doctor-badgering right-to-lifers make your skin crawl?

Then perhaps you'll understand what drove me to write *Ken's Guide to the Bible*.

I'm no religious scholar, and I'm certainly no Bible-razzing Satanist. But I *am* curious, and I wanted to know what in the Bible makes people so crazy. So I read it. And I was bug-eyed. Insane visions, twisted morals, greed, and bloodlust fill its pages. It's clear that those who champion the Bible as a guide to "family values" have only skimmed its surface, and those who use the Bible to push their religious and political agendas are keeping its weird parts under wraps.

This is not right. And this is what *Ken's Guide to the Bible* will fix.

Ken's Guide to the Bible is a map to the Good Book's bad secrets, a leveler of the scriptural playing field, a handy reference that flags everything in the Bible that those in the know don't want you to see. It debunks Bible myths that have circulated since God-knows-when and it gives quick, easy-to-grasp overviews of the Bible's books, major concepts, and outstanding personalities.

Ken's Guide to the Bible recognizes that the Bible has good content as well as bad. Many of Jesus' ethical and moral teachings are praiseworthy, as are four-fifths of the Ten Commandments and an occasional maxim from the prophets and the apostles. Despite the best efforts of organized religion to smother these messages with hoodoo embellishments and mystical rituals or to drag them down with the ridiculous notion that *everything* in the Bible is equally valid, they remain commendable and worth considering.

But you already know those lessons. What you need is a guide to the stuff that's been swept under the rug.

The Good Book has been coasting for years on good PR, fostered by those with an orthodox theology and made possible by Your and My ignorance of things biblical.

Wise up. Stop being a Bible bonehead. Read this guide.

And the next street-corner moralist who hassles you will wish he hadn't.

BASIC STUFF

The Bible isn't *a* book but is a *collection* of books—with around twenty letters thrown in as well. Any attempt to read it cover to cover usually proves aggravating, as many Bible books repeat what others have already described, and usually not in chronological order.

The Old Testament comprises the sacred literature (the "Scriptures") of Judaism, while the Old and New comprise the sacred literature of Christianity. The word "testament" is roughly equal to "covenant," which is roughly equal to "agreement" or "deal." Thus the Old Testament follows the old covenant, or deal, made between God and the people of Israel, while the New Testament follows the new deal made between God and the Christians, via Jesus. The Old Testament reached its final form around 150 B.C., the New around A.D. 100.

Each book in the Bible is divided into chapters and each chapter is divided into verses, though these divisions often don't divide thoughts or even sentences very cleanly. They are useful, however, for locating specific points in the Bible, and they are used that way in this guide. For instance, "Leviticus 5:23–31" means that the passage of the Bible under examination is in the book of Leviticus, fifth chapter, verses twenty-three through thirty-one.

Many people are under the impression that the *thees*, *thous*, and *thines* often associated with Bible scriptures reflect the nobility of their message. Actually, they reflect the nobility of Elizabethan English, the language in which the King James Version of the Bible—the only English version for almost three hundred years—was composed. The books of the Bible were originally written in Hebrew, Aramaic, and Greek and had existed for over a thousand years before the thees, thous, and thines were added. Jesus, Moses, and God never uttered a thee, thou, or thine in their lives.

WHICH BIBLE?

Odd as it may seem, before discussing the Bible the question must be asked, "Which Bible are we talking about?"

To the Jews, it's the Old Testament.

To most Protestants, it's the Old and New Testament.

To the Lutherans, Anglicans, Episcopalians, Roman Catholics, and the Eastern Orthodox, it's the Old and New Testament and the Apocrypha.

This guide takes the middle ground: yes New Testament, no Apocrypha.

The Bible books covered in this guide are presented as they are ordered in Christian Bibles.[†]

Another problem in Bible analysis (one never mentioned by Bible literalists) is that no two Bibles are exactly alike; each translation reflects the politics and religious doctrine of its sponsor. To minimize this bias, four Bibles were used as sources for this guide: the King James Version, the New Revised Standard Version, the Today's English ("Good News") Version, and the New International Version.

The Scriptures reprinted in this guide are from the New Revised Standard and New International versions. The language used in these Bibles is contemporary without being pandering. As lofty as Elizabethan English may be, its flowery prose can mask really weird messages.

KEN'S BIBLE-BUYING GUIDE

Ken's Guide to the Bible has been written to stand on its own, but some readers may want to refer to an actual Bible as they read it. Which Bible should you trust? Here is Ken's "litmus test" verse for ascertaining a Bible's politics:

[†] **Old Testament**
Genesis; Exodus; Leviticus; Numbers; Deuteronomy; Joshua; Judges; Ruth; I Samuel; II Samuel; I Kings; II Kings; I Chronicles; II Chronicles; Ezra; Nehemiah; Esther; Job; Psalms; Proverbs; Ecclesiastes; Song of Songs; Isaiah; Jeremiah; Lamentations; Ezekiel; Daniel; Hosea; Joel; Amos; Obadiah; Jonah; Micah; Nahum; Habakkuk; Zephaniah; Haggai; Zechariah; Malachi

New Testament
Matthew; Mark; Luke; John; Acts; Romans; I Corinthians; II Corinthians; Galatians; Ephesians; Philippians; Colossians; I Thessalonians; II Thessalonians; I Timothy; II Timothy; Titus; Philemon; Hebrews; James; I Peter; II Peter; I John; II John; III John; Jude; Revelation

✝ Ezekiel 23:20

New International Bible: "There she lusted after her lovers, whose genitals were like those of donkeys and whose emission was like that of horses."

New Revised Standard Bible: "She lusted after her paramours there, whose members were like those of donkeys and whose emission was like that of stallions."

King James Bible: "She dotes upon their paramours, whose flesh is as the flesh of asses, and whose issue is like the issue of horses."

Good News Bible: "She was filled with lust for oversexed men who had all the lustfulness of donkeys or stallions."

THINGS THAT AREN'T IN THE BIBLE

Over the past two-thousand-plus years many Bible stories have acquired a gummy coating of legend. Add to that the ritualistic baggage of the Catholic church and the modern tendency to ascribe anything that sounds old (such as quotes from Shakespeare) to the Bible, and the Bible has wound up as a dump for a lot of ill-conceived history and mythology. Here are some things that are not in the Bible:

✝ The people of Israel building pyramids
✝ Moses breaking the heart of his Pharaoh dad
✝ Solomon and the queen of Sheba having an affair
✝ Black Jesus
✝ Jesus and Mary Magdalene having an affair
✝ Jesus carrying lambs
✝ People waving palm branches
✝ Christians being killed in a Roman arena
✝ The archangel Gabriel blowing a horn
✝ Saint Peter standing at the pearly gates of heaven
✝ Anyone selling their soul to the Devil

- ✝ Any mention of guardian angels, original sin, holy communion, a sacred heart, a seventh heaven, the evil eye, the stations of the cross, the Immaculate Conception, Easter, Christmas, halos, nuns, monks, friars, popes, cardinals, bleeding statues, rosary beads, or people with ashes on their foreheads
- ✝ Any mention of venal or mortal sins
- ✝ Any veneration of relics
- ✝ Any condemnation of abortion
- ✝ Any reference to people becoming angels in heaven
- ✝ Cleopatra
- ✝ Mormons

THE BIBLE'S TOP TEN INFLUENTIAL CHARACTERS

To understand the Bible you have to understand its principal players. They're a scary and screwed-up bunch, but it wouldn't be a Good Book without a good cast of characters.

- ✝ **God** (He, Him, I Am, Jealous, King of Kings, Lord of lords) The first nonreproducible god in human history. Bloodthirsty and vengeful, despite the claims of New Testament writers. Excels at killing people. The scariest thing in the Bible.
- ✝ **Jesus** (Son of God, Lamb of God, the Word, the Messiah, the light of the world) A quick-witted, intelligent, articulate, earnest teacher who came to believe that he was the Son of God. The first man in recorded history to preach selflessness as the key to spirituality (if you ignore Buddha). Lived and died in Judea, roughly 7 B.C. to A.D. 29.
- ✝ **The apostle Paul** (Saul of Tarsus, the-apostle-to-the-Gentiles, St. Paul) Responsible, much more than Jesus, for

Christianity. His reworkings of Jesus' teachings spawned the Catholic church and continue to confuse most of humanity today.

- **Abraham** (Abram) The original testament/covenant/deal was struck between God and Abraham. God gave Abraham the divine right to settle in the land of Canaan (the "promised land," later renamed Israel), and in return Abraham promised that he and his descendents (the Israelites) would forever worship God.
- **Moses** The Jesus of the Old Testament. Also the closest thing to a buddy that God ever had. God chose Moses to lead the Israelites out of Egypt and into the promised land.
- **King David** The giant killer and the first king of Israel, but principally important because God liked him. After his death, it gradually became Judaic dogma that one of David's descendents would be the Messiah.
- **The ark of the covenant** (the ark of the testimony, the ark of God) The box that held the ten commandments and the scariest thing ever built by humankind. Second only to God in its viciousness and killing power.
- **Isaiah** The most verbose of the Old Testament prophets and the one quoted most often by Jesus and his followers when they wanted to justify Jesus' claim to Messiahhood.
- **The apostle John** (John-son-of-Zebedee, John the Beloved, St. John the Divine) Undistinguished during Jesus' lifetime, but his writings have provided our most popular images of the crucifixion and the Final Judgment.
- **The Devil** (Satan, Beelzebub, the dragon, the Old One, the fallen angel) Despite his importance to Christian fundamentalists, the Devil barely makes the top ten in the Bible's pantheon of movers and shakers. He always loses.

EASY-REFERENCE ICONS

Ken's Guide to the Bible employs graphic icons to help you quickly locate its most popular categories.

WEIRDNESS
When an event or a philosophy is incomprehensible even by Bible standards, this icon flags it.

BUNK
The sign of the bull signals things that many people erroneously believe about the Bible.

THE BIG PICTURE
Some of our most cherished Bible stories and scriptures look a lot different when they're viewed in context.

READ THIS AGAIN
Things to think about, despite this guide's best efforts to numb your higher brain functions.

DIVINE WRATH
God tortures and kills people with remarkable consistency, as this icon's frequent appearances testify.

HOLY DISTORTION
The crucified pretzel marks where New Testament writers have twisted sublime messages into self-serving theology.

BLOOD 'N' GUTS
If it isn't God killing people, it's people killing people.

FAMILY VALUES
The hellish spawn of today are only following the examples set down in the Good Book.

GENDER BASHING
From Eve (Genesis) to the great whore (Revelation), women usually get the blame whenever something goes wrong in the Bible.

SEX
The Bible's got lots of it.

CHRISTIAN ARROGANCE
Who's got the best religion in the world? You-know-who, and God have mercy on those who disagree.

KEN'S TWO CENTS' WORTH
Ken's sledgehammer prose is as biased as any religious diatribe. Here, at least, he admits it.

Welcome to

THE OLD TESTAMENT

The **Old Testament** is made up of thirty-nine separate books, written by different authors of different abilities at different times. These books can be divided into three groups: the first seventeen books are historical and, roughly, chronological; the middle five are either poetic or philosophic; and the last seventeen are prophetic.

IN THE BEGINNING . . .

The book of **Genesis** is the Old Testament's first and one of its best. It covers a lot of territory, has a wide cast of characters, and boasts enough sci-fi elements to keep things interesting. Many of the Bible's best-known stories are in Genesis: Adam and Eve, Cain and Abel, Noah and the flood, the tower of Babel, Sodom and Gomorrah. The latter half of the book follows the lineage of Abraham, Isaac, Jacob, and Jacob's sons, who eventually become the fathers of the twelve tribes of Israel.

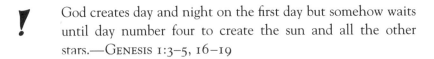 God creates day and night on the first day but somehow waits until day number four to create the sun and all the other stars.—GENESIS 1:3–5, 16–19

God repeatedly refers to Himself as "us," though why (and why only in Genesis) is never explained.—GENESIS 1:26; 3:22; 11:7

ADAM AND HIS FAMILY

 The Bible never reveals what kind of forbidden fruit Adam and Eve ate. It could have been a banana.—GENESIS 3:1–6

According to the Bible, the only "knowledge" imparted by the forbidden fruit is that the nude human body is embarrassing.—GENESIS 3:7

 Adam was not kicked out of the garden of Eden because he ate the forbidden fruit. A nervous God ejects Adam because He fears that His now-enlightened creation will eat fruit from a *second* tree—the tree of life—and that once he does, he will become immortal.—GENESIS 3:22–23

 The "mark of Cain" isn't a stigma, it's a protection. God puts it on killer Cain to warn away those who would otherwise avenge Abel's death.—GENESIS 4:13–15

 Cain killed Abel because God liked Abel more than Cain. Why? Cain was a farmer and all he could sacrifice to bloodthirsty God was plants. Abel was a herdsman and he could slaughter animals.—GENESIS 4:2–5

Jared, grandfather of Methuselah, lives only seven years less than his eponymous grandson (962 years vs. Methuselah's

969), but all for naught; no one today ever calls an old man a "Jared."—GENESIS 5:20, 27

God's sons come down from heaven and have sex with earth women.—GENESIS 6:1–2, 4

If you believe that Jesus wasn't a son of God (although *he* certainly believed that he was), then he wasn't related to the lusty "sons of God" in Genesis 6. But God does have sons, and they have come down from heaven and had sex with earth women.

"There were giants in the earth in those days. . . ." (Genesis 6:4) So it says in the King James and the Good News Bibles. Creationists like to cite this verse as proof that the earth was inhabited by a race of titanic people before the Flood. However, the ancient Hebrew word that has been translated as "giants" is "Nephilim" and no one is really sure what Nephilim means (the New Revised Standard and the New International Bibles leave it untranslated for this reason). Nephilim could simply mean exceptionally strong warriors or "very important people." In the 385-year-old King James Bible, this mistake is acceptable. In the five-year-old Good News Bible, it smacks of fundamentalist favoritism.

Noah
Noah is five hundred years old when he fathers his first child.—GENESIS 5:32

God tells Noah that He intends to kill nearly every living creature on earth because the world has become too violent. —GENESIS 6:13

Fundamentalist archaeologists who occasionally scour Mount Ararat looking for pieces of Noah's ark should reread their

Bibles. The scripture doesn't say that the ark beached on Mount Ararat but rather on "the mountains of Ararat"—that is, on an unnamed mountain in the kingdom of Ararat—and the Bible doesn't say where Ararat is.—GENESIS 8:4

Noah gets drunk on wine from his vineyard and passes out with his genitals exposed. Ham, his son, accidently sees him. When Noah awakens and finds out, he punishes Ham by making Ham's youngest son a slave.—GENESIS 9:20–27

An obviously nervous God confuses the languages of the inhabitants of Babel (and, consequently, of the whole earth) when He realizes that if all humans speak the same language, they'll be able to accomplish things without God. "Look, they are one people, and they have all one language; and this is only the beginning of what they will do; nothing that they propose to do will now be impossible for them."—GENESIS 11:1–9

Abraham is married to Sarah, his beautiful half-sister. He curries favor (and grows rich) by allowing the Pharaoh of Egypt to have sex with her. He tells the Pharaoh that Sarah is his sister. He fails to mention that she is also his wife.—GENESIS 12:10–20

God makes a covenant with Abraham and demands that he—and all of his descendents—seal the deal by being circumcised (GENESIS 17:10). God never explains why slicing away the foreskin of the penis is important, and it seems particularly strange in light of the Bible's repeated tirades against human genital exposure. What good is a distinguishing self-mutilation that no one is allowed to see?

After fleeing the destruction of Sodom, Lot and his two virgin daughters end up living in a cave. The daughters worry that now they'll never find husbands and have children. So they get their father drunk and have sex with him.—GENESIS 19:30–36

Jacob and His Family
Jacob and his extensive family, from whom the nation of Israel descends, are some of the sleaziest, trashiest people in the Bible. Some examples of their bad behavior:

Jacob cheats Esau, his dumb twin brother, and brazenly lies to Isaac, his blind, old father, so that he can become the chief heir of Isaac's property.—GENESIS 25:29–34; 27

Jacob wants to have sex with lovely Rachel (his first cousin), but her father demands seven years of labor in exchange. Jacob

sex

Saucy Rachel has the hots for Jacob, and wallflower Leah wants a piece of the action, too. Jacob later boffs them both.

does his time, and then on the wedding night Rachel's father tricks Jacob into having sex with (and thereby marrying) Leah, Rachel's ugly sister (another first cousin). Rachel's father then gladly gives Rachel to Jacob as a second wife—in exchange for seven more years of labor.—GENESIS 29:15–30

 Rachel and Leah battle for Jacob's favor by giving him their maids as sex partners.—GENESIS 30:1–11

 Rachel makes a barter deal with Leah: a night of sex with Jacob for some mandrake plants.—GENESIS 30:14–16

 Jacob becomes rich by cheating his father-in-law out of his best sheep and goats. Jacob then skips town with his booty and his women and tells Rachel and Leah that his prosperity is an act of God.—GENESIS 30:31–34, 37–42; 31:4–5, 8–9

 God has a wrestling match with Jacob and loses. To honor the occasion, God changes Jacob's name to "Israel."—GENESIS 32:24–30

The prince of the city of Shechem rapes Jacob's daughter and then becomes enamored of her and decides that he wants to marry her. Jacob's sons insist that the only way that they'll permit this is if the prince and every man in his city is circumcised. The prince readily agrees, and while he and his male citizens are still recovering from their painful operations, Jacob's sons attack the city, plundering and pillaging, enslaving the women, and killing all of the men.—GENESIS 34

 The "sin of Onan" is not masturbation. Onan sinned not because he "spilled his semen on the ground" but because, by doing so, he didn't impregnate his sister-in-law—which is what God specifically wanted. God kills Onan.—GENESIS 38:1–10

Judah, one of Jacob's sons, has sex with his daughter-in-law after she tricks him into thinking that she's a prostitute.—GENESIS 38:11–19

Joseph, another of Jacob's sons, declares that God has made him "lord of all Egypt" and refuses to give grain to its starving people unless they sell themselves into slavery to his master. His master is Pharaoh, not God.—GENESIS 45:9; 47:13–21

Jacob gives Joseph the status of eldest son after he discovers that Reuben, his real eldest son, has had sex with his mistress (GENESIS 35:22). Jacob brands Reuben as "unstable" (GENESIS 49:4). The Bible later mentions that Reuben "defiled his father's bed" (I CHRONICLES 5:1) and leaves it at that.

Joseph turns his dead father, Jacob, the namesake of Israel, into a mummy.—GENESIS 50:1–3

MOSES AND THE EXODUS

Exodus, Leviticus, Numbers, and **Deuteronomy** tell the story of Moses and of the people of Israel, Jacob's descendents, who are thrown out of Egypt and wander in the Sinai Peninsula for forty years. Moses is the closest thing in the Old Testament to Jesus, though he's as capable of bloodthirsty fanaticism as any of his contemporaries. Unlike Cecil B. DeMille's movie *The Ten Commandments*, the Bible often depicts Moses as a meek man—he repeatedly asks that his brother, Aaron, do his public speaking—yet the people of Israel owe him their lives. Without Moses' frequent pleas for forgiveness, God would have killed His chosen people ten times over.

God orders Moses to Egypt to lead the people of Israel out of bondage. Then, for reasons that are never made clear, He abruptly decides to kill him. Moses' wife saves him by rubbing his feet with the bloody foreskin of his son.—EXODUS 4:24–26

The Bible never reveals what kind of "sea" that Moses (with a little help from God) parted. It leads us to *infer* that it was the Red Sea, setting the scene by stating, "...God led the people...toward the Red Sea" (EXODUS 13:18) and then afterward, Moses led Israel "...from the Red Sea" (EXODUS 15:22), but these only use the Red Sea as a directional marker before and after the event. (They could just as accurately have been written, "God led the people southeastward.") Nowhere in Exodus 14's description of the parting does the Bible mention anything more specific than a "sea"—even though it has fifteen references in which to do so.

The Bible does offer one verse that apparently links Moses' miracle to the Red Sea: "...[The Pharaoh's] picked officers were sunk in the Red Sea" (EXODUS 15:4). However, most modern Bibles add a tiny footnote to this verse indicating that the original Hebrew translates to "sea of reeds," not "Red Sea."

The people of Israel battle the people of Amalek. Moses watches from a hill; whenever he raises his hand, the people of Israel win. Unfortunately, Moses is eighty years old, and whenever he gets tired and lowers his hand, the people of Israel lose. Moses' two companions solve this problem (and win the battle) by sitting Moses on a rock and holding up both of his hands.—EXODUS 17:10–13

God proclaims that none of the people of Israel can as much as *touch* Mount Sinai while He's on it. "Any who touch the mountain shall be put to death," God decrees. "They shall be stoned or shot with arrows; whether animal or human being, they shall not live."—EXODUS 19:12–14

The Commandments of God

When God gives Moses His commandments on Mt. Sinai—which the Bible prefers to call "ordinances" or simply "the law"—He doesn't stop at ten. In fact, the total reaches nearly six hundred. Some of the others that aren't usually mentioned:

God instructs Moses that no altar to God should have steps; people ascending steps might expose their genitals.—Exodus 20:26

God tells Moses that a man who beats his servant or maid should be punished only if the victim dies. If the victim is only incapacitated for a day or two, no punishment is necessary. After all, God notes, it's his money.—Exodus 21:20–21

"You shall not permit a female sorcerer to live."—Exodus 22:18 (also Leviticus 20:27)

"Whoever curses father or mother shall be put to death."—Exodus 21:17 (also Leviticus 20:9)

"Anyone who has sexual relations with an animal must be put to death."—Exodus 22:19 (also Leviticus 20:15–16)

"Whoever does any work on the Sabbath day shall be put to death."—Exodus 31:15 (also 35:2)

"One who blasphemes the name of the Lord shall be put to death."—Leviticus 24:16

Though the Bible is a bloody book, those who justify their own brutality by citing its "eye for eye" passage are taking it out of context. God's approval for such action is pinpoint specific: it only applies 1) when men who are fighting 2) hit a pregnant woman 3) who then miscarries 4) and is seriously injured as a result.—EXODUS 21:22–25

Moses performs the first Bible baptism. It isn't done with water, but with ox blood.—EXODUS 24:5–8

 God learns about the golden calf and is angry. Moses has to talk Him out of killing all of the people of Israel. Instead, Moses suggests that those who didn't worship the golden calf prove their loyalty by killing those closest to them—neighbors, friends, relatives, children—who did. Roughly three thousand are butchered. God still isn't appeased; He unleashes a plague on the survivors.—EXODUS 32:7–14, 25–35

 God warns Moses that anyone who sees His face will die. But as a reward, He allows Moses to see His back.—EXODUS 33:18–23

God tells Moses His name is really "Jealous."—EXODUS 34:14

 Moses is forced to wear a veil in public; talking to God has made his face glow.—EXODUS 34:29–35

Charlton Heston didn't wear a bag over his head after he talked with God, but the real Moses did.

The Ark of the Covenant

The books of the Old Testament that document the building of the ark of the covenant (the cedar chest–like thing pursued by Indiana Jones) depict God as a deity obsessed with detail, fond of blood, and pleased with the smell of burning meat. Over twenty chapters of Exodus and Leviticus describe in dry, excruciatingly minute detail the construction of the ark, its sheltering tent, and the gory rituals to be performed upon its altar:

"You shall lay your hand on the head of the offering and slaughter it . . . the priests shall dash the blood against all sides of the altar . . . you shall offer from the sacrifice of well-being, as an offering by fire made to the Lord the fat that covers the entrails and all the fat that is around the entrails; the two kidneys with the fat that is on them at the loins, and the appendage of the liver, which [you] shall remove with the kidneys . . . as an offering by fire of pleasing odor to the Lord."
—LEVITICUS 3:2–5

The ark became a kind of traveling safety deposit box, transporting the slabs of stone upon which God had inscribed His primary ten commandments. The people of Israel carried the ark with them as they wandered in the wilderness, following God, who went before them cloaked inside a pillar of clouds or fire. When God wanted the people of Israel to pitch camp, he would settle down over the ark and speak to Moses from a seat of pure gold set on top of it.

God tells Moses that Aaron and his sons must always wear underwear when they enter God's tent or else they will be killed.—EXODUS 28:42–43

God tells Moses that every time Moses takes a census, all of the people of Israel will have to pay a "ransom" that will go to the upkeep of God's tent. Otherwise, God will unleash a plague on them.—EXODUS 30:11–16

*Aaron's sons are charbroiled by the ark of God, which
has a nasty habit of killing people it doesn't like.*

 The ark burns two of Aaron's sons to death because their offerings to God are unauthorized.—LEVITICUS 10:1–2

 God tells the people of Israel that they cannot eat bats, but that grasshoppers and locusts are okay.—LEVITICUS 11:19–22

 God, perhaps remembering the antics of Jacob, forbids men from marrying sisters unless one of them is dead.—LEVITICUS 18:18

God forbids tattoos.—LEVITICUS 19:28

 God decrees that male homosexuals must be put to death. He says nothing about lesbians.—LEVITICUS 20:13

God decrees that His priests must be free of physical defects: they cannot be dwarfs, they cannot have "an itching disease or scabs" or "crushed testicles."—LEVITICUS 21:17–21

Chapters 13–15 of Leviticus are devoted exclusively to detailed descriptions of skin diseases and gross bodily fluids, such as pus, semen, and menstrual flow. This biblical field guide to personal hygiene contains advice such as: "When a woman has a discharge of blood that is her regular discharge from her body . . . whoever touches anything upon which she sits shall wash his clothes and bathe in water. . . ." and "The person who has the leprous disease shall wear torn clothes and let the hair of his head be disheveled; and he shall cover his upper lip and cry out, 'Unclean! Unclean!'"

The nicest words ever attributed to God, "Love your neighbor as yourself" (LEVITICUS 19:18), have been significantly improved by taking them out of context. In context, it's apparent that the "neighbor" God refers to is a neighboring Israelite.

According to God, any man who suspects his wife of adultery must bring her into God's tent, where a priest will make her drink dirty water. ". . . The water," God explains, "shall enter into her and cause bitter pain, and her womb shall discharge, her uterus drop, and the woman shall become an execration among her people." Unless, of course, the woman is innocent, in which case "she shall be immune and be able to conceive children."—NUMBERS 5:11–31

Some of the people of Israel grow tired of eating manna every day and ask God to give them meat. God grumbles but sends them a flock of quail. Then He gets mad anyway and kills the meat eaters with a plague.—NUMBERS 11:4–5, 31–34

Moses' sister, Miriam, complains that her prophesies are just as good as her brother's. God responds by turning her into a leper.—NUMBERS 12:1–10

 "When the Israelites were in the wilderness, they found a man gathering sticks on the sabbath day. Those who found him gathering sticks brought him to Moses, Aaron, and to the whole congregation. They put him in custody because it was not clear what should be done to him.

"Then the Lord said to Moses, 'The man shall be put to death. All the congregation shall stone him outside the camp.' The whole congregation brought him outside the camp and stoned him to death, just as the Lord had commanded Moses."—NUMBERS 15:32–36

 Two-hundred-fifty of Israel's community leaders challenge the authority of Moses and Aaron. God kills all 250 and opens a pit into hell into which their three leaders and all the members of their families are swallowed alive. When the people of Israel complain that killing the people of Israel isn't right, God sends a plague that kills nearly fifteen thousand more.—NUMBERS 16

 The men of Israel mingle with the women of Midian, who tempt them into worshipping a rival god (Baal) atop Mount Peor. God is once again ready to kill everybody. Happily, Eleazar, one of Aaron's replacement sons, impales a man of Israel and his Midianite girlfriend with a spear in front of God's tent. God is appeased, and the plague He sends only kills twenty-four thousand.—NUMBERS 25:1–9

 The Lord commands the men of Israel to slay the Midianites. This they do, with gusto, killing every man, plundering and pillaging, and taking for slaves all the women and children.

Nevertheless, when they return to camp Moses is not pleased. "Have you allowed all the women to live?" he asks them. "...Kill every male among the little ones. And kill every woman who has known a man by sleeping with him. But all the young girls who have not known a man by sleeping with him, keep alive for yourselves."—NUMBERS 31:1 18

Many Sunday-school veterans know the story of Balaam and his God-fearing, talking ass; it's the only nice animal story in the Old Testament (NUMBERS 22:21–34). Few know that Balaam is deliberately hunted down and butchered in the Midianite massacre.

Balaam remains an object of frequent, repeated scorn throughout the Bible, even though he was actually obedient to and fearful of God. His perpetual damnation springs from one accusation by Moses in Numbers 31 that it was on Balaam's advice that the Midianite women seduced the Israelite men, even though the Bible otherwise makes no mention of this incident. No matter: Balaam bashing is one of the Bible's most consistent themes, continuing even into Revelation, the last book in the New Testament.

"I see him, but not now; I behold him, but not near—a star shall come out of Jacob; and a scepter shall rise out of Israel...." (NUMBERS 24:17) This passage is often cited by Christians as proof that Jesus' coming was foretold even in the time of Moses. What the Christians don't say is that this prediction comes from the mouth of Bible-damned Balaam.

"If your very own brother, or your son or daughter, or the wife you love, or your closest friend secretly entices you, saying, 'Let us go and worship other gods....' Show him no pity. Do not spare him or shield him. Your hand must be the first in putting him to death, and then the hands of all the people. Stone him to death because he tried to turn you away from the Lord your God. . . ."—DEUTERONOMY 13:6, 8–9

"If someone has a stubborn and rebellious son who will not obey his father and mother, who does not heed them when they discipline him, then his father and his mother shall take hold of him and bring him out to the elders of his town. . . . They shall say to the elders of his town, 'This son of ours is stubborn and rebellious. He will not obey us. He is a glutton and a drunkard.' Then all the men of the town shall stone him to death."—DEUTERONOMY 21:18–21

God forbids cross-dressing.—DEUTERONOMY 22:5

"Suppose a man marries a woman, but after going in to her, he dislikes her and makes up charges against her, slandering her by saying, 'I married this woman; but when I lay with her, I did not find evidence of her virginity.' The father of the young woman and her mother shall then submit the evidence of the young woman's virginity to the elders of the city at the gate. The father of the young woman shall say to the elders: 'I gave my daughter in marriage to this man but he dislikes her; now he has made up charges against her, saying, "I did not find evidence of your daughter's virginity." But here is the evidence of my daughter's virginity.' Then they shall spread out the cloth before the elders of the town. The elders of that town shall take the man and punish him; they shall fine him one hundred shekels of silver (which they shall give to the young woman's father) because he has slandered a virgin of Israel. She shall remain his wife; he shall not be permitted to divorce her as long as he lives.

"If, however, this charge is true, that evidence of the young woman's virginity was not found, then they shall

bring the young woman out to the entrance of her father's house and the men of her town shall stone her to death. . . ."
—Deuteronomy 22:13–21

God bans from His chosen people any man with crushed testicles or a severed penis.—Deuteronomy 23:1

God forbids His chosen people from lending money at interest to each other but adds that lending money at interest to foreigners is okay.—Deuteronomy 23:19–20

"If men get into a fight with one another, and the wife of one intervenes to rescue her husband from the grip of his opponent by reaching out and seizing his genitals, you shall cut off her hand; show her no pity."—Deuteronomy 25:11–12

When the twelve tribes of Israel finally reach the Promised Land, they discover that it is already filled with people. These inhabitants might have posed a problem to some, but not to God. He orders the people of Israel—now under the leadership of Joshua—to kill them.—Deuteronomy 20:10–18

THE PROMISED LAND

The book of **Joshua** opens with what could be called the "religious cleansing" of the Promised Land. After forty years in the wilderness, the people of Israel had become a mobile attack force of thousands of zealots willing to massacre almost anyone at God's behest. (And they'd better: God has left an extensive—and explicit—list of the atrocities He'll inflict on anyone who doesn't follow orders.—Deuteronomy 28:15–68)

Jericho is the most famous of Israel's many bloody conquests, but it is otherwise typical: Israel attacked it, not the other way around (in fact, Jericho's people were cowering behind its walls); the city was destroyed, all of its inhabitants were butchered, and then the people of Israel divvied up its booty and moved on.

 "When Israel had finished slaughtering all the inhabitants of Ai in the open wilderness where they pursued them, and when all of them to the very last had fallen by the edge of the sword, all Israel returned to Ai and attacked it with the edge of the sword. The total of those who fell that day, both men and women, was twelve thousand—all the people of Ai."— JOSHUA 8:24–25

 In order that Joshua might have good light to thoroughly butcher the Amorites, God makes the sun stand still for an entire day.—JOSHUA 10:12–14

 "So Joshua defeated the whole land.... He left no one remaining, but utterly destroyed all that breathed, as the Lord God of Israel commanded."—JOSHUA 10:40

After the death of Joshua, the people of Israel lose their cohesion and are led by a series of tribal leaders, or **Judges**. These lesser lights often accomplish their God-approved goals through cunning, rather than by brute force:

Ehud flatters the fat king of Moab with presents, then confides to him that, "I have a message from God for you." He plunges a sword into his gut.—JUDGES 3:20–22

Deborah, the strongest positive-role-model female figure in the entire Bible, defeats general Sisera of the Canaanites with the help of another woman, Ja'el, who drives a tent peg into his skull.—JUDGES 4:17–22

Gideon defeats the Midianite army with only three hundred men by confusing the Midianites with torches and trumpet blasts. The three hundred are handpicked by God after they display an aptitude for lapping water like dogs.—JUDGES 7:1–22

Despite these occasional lapses into forethought, most of the judges exhibit the standard Old Testament traits of reckless bloodletting and mindless genocide:

Gideon's son, Abimelech, rises to power by killing his seventy older brothers (one has to admire his stick-to-itiveness). God, however, punishes (and humiliates) him for this unsanctioned butchery by having a woman drop a millstone on his head.—JUDGES 9:50–57

Jephthah promises God that if He will make him victorious in battle, he will turn whoever first greets him afterward into a burnt offering. God fulfills His end of the bargain, and when Jephthah comes home he is greeted by—his virgin daughter. God, who has in past chapters decried the horror of child sacrifice and who has used it to justify His bloody lack of mercy toward Israel's neighbors (see DEUTERONOMY 18:9–12), sits back and watches her burn.—JUDGES 11:30–39

SAMSON

Samson is depicted in the Bible as a quasi barbarian, yet he's also credited as being one of the judges of Israel. How he rose to that position, and who decided that he could be trusted to judge anything, is not explained.

Hotheaded Samson takes a Philistine wife. She immediately humiliates him by revealing the answer to a riddle he's posed to his wedding guests. Samson pays off the riddle wager by robbing (and killing) thirty innocent people, then gives his bride to his best man, and stalks off. After a few weeks he comes back and wants to have sex with her, but her father refuses. ("I was so sure you thoroughly hated her that I gave her to your friend.") Samson, enraged, burns the Philistines' grain and olive orchards. The Philistines, in return, burn his former bride and father-in-law.—JUDGES 14:10–20; 15:1–6

 One of Israel's twelve tribes, the Danites, needs a place to settle. Guided by God, they discover the well-to-do city of Laish, inhabited by peaceful and unsuspecting people. The Danites destroy the city, slaughter the people, and settle down among the ruins.—JUDGES 18:1–2, 7–10, 27–28

 An unnamed Israelite priest and his mistress spend the night in the city of Gibeah, where they are besieged by the men of the city who want to have sex with the priest. The priest, ever resourceful, throws his mistress out to the men. She is raped and abused for hours. In the morning, the priest retrieves the woman (the Bible is unclear whether she is dead or merely unconscious), takes her home, then hacks her into twelve pieces and sends the body parts to the leaders of the twelve tribes of Israel. The ensuing war against Gibeah kills over sixty-five thousand.—JUDGES 19:11–30; 20:1–46

After the above slaughter, only six hundred men of the tribe of Benjamin are left alive (the Benjaminites defended Gibeah). The other eleven tribes of Israel are in a quandary: they can't let one of Israel's tribes die out, but they also promised God that they wouldn't give their daughters in marriage to the loser Benjaminites. A happy solution is found: the eleven tribes destroy the city of Jabash Gilead (whose inhabitants had failed to participate in the Gibeah carnage) and the four hundred virgins left alive are given to the Benjaminites. This still leaves the men of Benjamin two hundred short, so the elders of Israel order them to go to the nearby city of Shiloh and steal enough virgins to make up the difference.—JUDGES 20:47–48; 21

The book of **Ruth** is a short one, and it serves as a breather in the Bible's brutal historical narrative. It tells a simple, gentle story of compassion and love and provides no grist for the mill of a guide such as this.

THE KINGDOM OF ISRAEL

The books of **Samuel**, **Kings**, and **Chronicles** mark the passing of power from the judges to the kings of Israel (and, eventually, of Judah as well). They are filled with accounts of endless, bloody civil wars and gore-filled coups and counter-coups. God frequently provides tactical advice.

Eli, the high priest of the Israelites, is thunderstruck when he hears that the ark of God has been captured by the Philistines. He thus becomes the only person in the Bible to die by falling out of a chair.—I SAMUEL 4:16–18

The Philistines quickly discover that the ark of God is no prize; it inflicts plagues of rats and tumors wherever they take it. After seven months the Philistines ship it back to the Israelites, along with offerings of golden rats and tumors. —I SAMUEL 5:6–12; 6:1–12

The ark of God arrives in the city of Beth Shemesh, which rejoices in its good fortune. Some of its men decide to take a peek inside the ark; the ark immediately kills them. The survivors, no longer joyful, ship the ark to the neighboring city of Kiriath Jearim.—I SAMUEL 6:13–21

In the King James Version of the Bible, God's murderous vengeance in the above incident leaves fifty thousand dead. In the Good News version, the total is reduced to seventy.

The Israelites are about to be attacked by the Philistines when God confuses the Philistine forces by yelling at them. The Israelites win.—I SAMUEL 7:10

Saul, the first God-anointed king of Israel, ensures that Israel's people will follow him into battle by threatening to kill all of their oxen.—I SAMUEL 11:5–7

Untimely Justice

As the soap opera of Israel's many kings unfolds, God's clear, if bloody, ideology becomes muddled. He breaks His "children shall not be put to death for their fathers" law (II CHRONICLES 25:4 et al) frequently, creating a weird continuum in which the wrongdoers often get off scot free and the good who follow suffer.

God orders Saul to destroy the people of Amalek because they'd had the audacity, several hundred years previously, to fight against Israel (and almost win; remember Moses' tired arms?). "Now go and attack Amalek and utterly destroy all that they have; do not spare them, but kill both man and woman, child and infant, ox and sheep, camel and donkey."—I SAMUEL 15:2–3

Saul captures King Agag (of the recently destroyed kingdom of Amalek) and brings him to Gilgal. There the king meets Samuel, the high priest of Israel. Agag is happy that Saul has spared his life and is pleased to meet Samuel. What he doesn't know is that the old priest (and God) frown upon Saul's leniency. Samuel hacks Agag to pieces.—I SAMUEL 15:32–33

David

The Old Testament describes future king David, one of the most bloodstained characters in Bible history, as having "beautiful eyes."—I SAMUEL 16:12

Despite what you might have learned in Sunday school, David did not kill Goliath with a stone. The messy truth is that David only knocked Goliath unconscious; he killed him with Goliath's own sword and then hacked off his head. —I SAMUEL 17:51

David, future king of Israel, hoists the drippy head of Goliath aloft for God's approval.

43

To prove his love for Saul's daughter, David brings the king the foreskins of a hundred slain Philistines.—I SAMUEL 18:27

Nabal, a rich businessman, refuses to give food to David and his men. David decides to slaughter Nabal and his family, but Nabal's wife, Abigail, runs to David and begs forgiveness. David relents, God kills Nabal, and Abigail is free to marry David.—I SAMUEL 25

David learns from an escaped Israelite soldier that King Saul is dead, having fallen on his own sword rather than die at the hands of the Philistines. Unfortunately, he didn't fall on it very well, and he had to beg the Israelite soldier to finish the job. David rewards the obedient soldier by immediately having him killed. "Your blood be on your own head," David declares, "for your own mouth has testified against you, saying, 'I have killed the Lord's anointed.' "—II SAMUEL 1:2–16

The last surviving son of Saul is beheaded by two of his captains, who then triumphantly carry the head to David. The two captains are jubilant, as the path is now clear for David's ascension to the throne. The captains obviously hadn't heard the story of the Israelite soldier; David immediately has them killed.—II SAMUEL 4:5–12

 King David decides to move the ark of God to the city of Jerusalem, Israel's new capital. While the ark is being transported, one of the oxen that are pulling it stumbles, and one of the drivers, named Uzzah, instinctively reaches out to steady it. The ark kills him instantly. David decides that moving the ark into his new capital maybe isn't such a good idea.—II SAMUEL 6:2–10; I CHRONICLES 13:6–13

The ark of God finally arrives in Jerusalem. King David (his fears laid to rest) leads the parade, "leaping and dancing before the Lord." Michal, one of David's many wives (and a daughter of the dead King Saul) sees David's performance and upbraids him for it. God makes her infertile.—II Samuel 6:16, 20–23

Lusty King David breaks the seventh commandment by having sex with Bathsheba, the wife of one of his subjects. He then breaks the sixth commandment by arranging for Bathsheba's husband to be put in the front line of his latest war, where he is immediately killed. God is angry but accommodating. He kills David and Bathsheba's baby.—II Samuel 11:2–4, 14–27; 12:9–19

David and Bathsheba's second baby, conceived immediately after the death of their first, brings no objection from God. —II Samuel 12:24–25

The war in which Bathsheba's husband was killed (along with thousands of others) began when the king of the Ammonites shaved off half the beards of King David's emissaries. —II Samuel 10:1–5

David's son Amnon brutally rapes his half-sister Tamar. Another of David's sons, Absalom, finds out about the rape and comforts Tamar with these words: "Has that Amnon, your brother, been with you? Be quiet now, my sister; he is your brother. Don't take this thing to heart."—II Samuel 13:1–20

In retribution for dead King Saul's past excesses, God plagues the people of Israel with a three-year famine. This is unfair, and King David appeases God with an equally unfair solution: he authorizes the crucifixion of Saul's last two illegitimate sons and five of his grandsons.—II Samuel 21:1–9

King David is provoked into taking a census of Israel's population. The census angers God, who sees it as questioning His vow to make the people of Israel "as numerous as the stars of heaven." God punishes David (and throws off his count) by killing seventy thousand innocent Israelites with a pestilence. —I CHRONICLES 21:1–7, 14; 27:23–24 (also II SAMUEL 24:1–17)

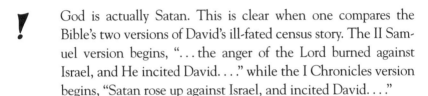

God is actually Satan. This is clear when one compares the Bible's two versions of David's ill-fated census story. The II Samuel version begins, ". . . the anger of the Lord burned against Israel, and He incited David. . . ." while the I Chronicles version begins, "Satan rose up against Israel, and incited David. . . ."

God refuses to let King David build a temple for God's ark because David has killed too many people.—I CHRONICLES 22:6–8

God conveniently forgets David's sins when He wants to dish out brutality to subsequent kings. ". . . You have not been like my servant David," He chides David's successors, "who kept My commandments and followed Me with all his heart, doing only that which was right in My sight. . . ."—I KINGS 14:8

King David flees Jerusalem when his son Absalom usurps the throne. On the way out of town, David is cursed by a man named Shimei, who calls him a "man of blood." Absalom is killed, David returns to power, and he makes a great show of promising Shimei that he won't be murdered. At least not right away.

Years later, on his deathbed, David orders his son Solomon to kill Shimei. Solomon, wise in the ways of shifting responsibility, orders Shimei to live in Jerusalem; if he leaves, "your blood shall be on your own head." (Like father like son: remember David and the hapless Israelite soldier?) It takes three years, but Shimei eventually lets down his guard and leaves Jerusalem to chase after two runaway slaves. Solomon has him killed.—II SAMUEL 16:5–13; 19:16–23; I KINGS 2:8–9, 36–46

Solomon and Sheba

The queen of Sheba visits Solomon and the two exchange gifts and royal pleasantries. That's it. No sex; not even a hint of it. The queen's visit lasts for thirteen verses, less than one-half of one Bible page.—I KINGS 10:1–13 (also II CHRONICLES 9:1–12)

The Bible never mentions the queen's race, but it's likely that she was an Arabian, not an African. Bible maps place Sheba on the site of the present nation of Yemen, and Yemen is in Arabia, not Africa.

Perhaps the belief that the queen of Sheba was black is rooted in another Bible book, The Song of Solomon. In it, an unnamed "bride" twice refers to herself as "black" in the King James Version, but these inexact references have been changed, in various modern Bibles, to "dark," "very dark," "tanned," and "swarthy."

People unaware of these changes may put the "black" "bride" together with "Solomon" and come up with a black queen of Sheba. But if they do, then they ignore the particulars given in the Scriptures, wherein Solomon is never described as even being attracted to the queen, let alone becoming her husband, and the bride is described as being a peasant girl.

Solomon marries the Pharaoh's daughter, an event notable for its lack of protest from God or the Bible.—I KINGS 3:1

To pay for all the gold and the expensive wood that Solomon needs to build God's temple (and Solomon's much larger palace), Solomon sells twenty Israelite cities to the godless King of Tyre. Again, no protest from God or the Bible, although the King of Tyre gripes that the cities aren't very good.—I KINGS 9:10-13

Solomon accumulates a thousand wives and mistresses. As frequently happens in the Old Testament, a woman—or, in this case, many women—lead their man away from the worship of God, and Solomon becomes a devotee of "abominations" such as Ashtoreth and Milcom and Chemosh. However, despite these repeated violations of Commandment #1, God does not punish Solomon. He punishes his innocent son.—I KINGS 11:1-12; NEHEMIAH 13:26-27

Kill Your Neighbor
After the death of Solomon, Israel refuses to accept the rule of his son and the nation is split into two kingdoms: Israel and Judah. As generation replaces generation, God supports whichever king is more submissive to Him, leading to chapters of confusion in which the Israelites are good guys on one page, bad guys on the next.

 Jeroboam is made the king of breakaway Israel and quickly turns to the worship of molten images. God takes a much dimmer view of Jeroboam's shenanigans than of Solomon's and pledges that every member of his family will be butchered and left to rot. Nevertheless, God finds something good in Jeroboam's son Abijah and shows His kindness by immediately killing the boy. At least, God explains, he will be buried.—I KINGS 14:1-13

 Greatest single slaughter in Bible history: Asa, the great-grandson of Solomon and the king of Judah (God-approved) battles Zerah the Ethiopian (God-disapproved). The entire Ethiopian army, one million men, dies.—II CHRONICLES 14:8-13

King Asa calls together all of the people of Judah and makes them swear to seek God and to swear that "whoever would not seek the Lord, the God of Israel, should be put to death, whether young or old, man or woman."—II Chronicles 15:9–15

King Jehoram, the grandson of Asa, does not meet with God's approval. God strikes him with an intestinal disease that takes two years to kill him, causing his bowels to slide out of his body, little by little. "He died in great agony," the Bible notes, "with no one's regret."—II Chronicles 21:18–20

The prophet Micaiah, apparently exempt from God's warning to Moses, becomes the first person since Moses to see God. He describes Him as sitting on a "throne" (the ark's gold seat?) but provides no other details. King Ahab throws him into prison.—I Kings 22:19, 26–27

Elijah and Elisha

The prophet Elijah and his successor, the prophet Elisha, roam the blasphemous Israel of the books of Kings and Chronicles. They are two of the creepiest characters in the Old Testament, men that one would *never* want to meet, who combine fundamentalist heavy-handedness with supernatural powers. Some examples:

Elijah becomes the first Bible-recorded human to raise another human from the dead.—I Kings 17:17–22

"[The king] sent to Elijah a captain with his company of fifty men. The captain went up to Elijah, who was sitting on the top of a hill, and said to him, 'Man of God, the king says, "Come down!"' Elijah answered the captain, 'If I am a man of God, may fire come down from heaven and consume you and your fifty men!' Then fire fell from heaven and consumed the captain and his men."—II KINGS 1:9–10

 Elijah parts the Jordan River by smacking it with his cloak. —II KINGS 2:7–8

 Elijah takes a trip in a whirlwind to meet God and thus becomes the only human in the Bible to go to heaven without dying.—II KINGS 2:11

Elijah is too busy riding a flaming chariot to heaven to notice that someone has swiped his river-splitting cloak.

 The author of Hebrews in the New Testament claims Enoch, father of Methuselah, also went to heaven without dying (HE-BREWS 11:5). This is apparently based on a too-literal reading of one sentence in the Old Testament. ("Enoch walked with God; then he was no more because God took him."—GENESIS 5:24)

*"Baldhead" Elisha uses his godlike powers to turn
some biblical brats into bear chow.*

"[Elisha] went up . . . to Bethel; and while he was going up on the way, some small boys came out of the city and jeered at him, saying, 'Go away, baldhead! Go away, baldhead!' When he turned and saw them, he cursed them in the name of the Lord. Then two she-bears came out of the woods and mauled forty-two of the boys."—II Kings 2:23–24

Elisha's servant, Gehazi, tricks one of Elisha's patrons into giving Gehazi a present. Elisha turns Gehazi—as well as all of his descendents—into lepers.—II Kings 5:20–27

Elisha tells the king of Samaria that the siege of his city will be lifted. One of the king's captains questions Elisha's prediction. The next day the siege is lifted, and the captain is crushed to death under waves of escaping citizens.—II Kings 7:1–2, 16–18

A dead man is accidentally interred in Elisha's tomb; he touches Elisha's bones and springs back to life. Elisha thus becomes the only dead person in the Bible to revive another dead person.—II KINGS 13:20–21

 God assures Elisha that the combined armies of Israel and Judah will have an easy victory over the army of Moab. The king of Moab, in dire straits, burns his oldest son as a sacrifice to Chemosh, the Moabite deity. The combined armies of Israel and Judah—and God—lose.—II KINGS 3:18–19, 26–27

 Jehu, God's latest anointed leader, kills both the king of Judah and the king of Israel and then proceeds to butcher all of the Israelite king's family members, friends, councillors, priests, relatives, etc. For good measure, he calls all of the worshippers of Baal to an assembly in Baal's temple ("I am going to hold a

Jezebel is the most uppity woman in the Bible, so her fate is particularly gruesome. Note the enthusiastic, hungry dogs.

great sacrifice for Baal") and kills all of them, too. God is pleased.—II KINGS 9:21–24, 27; 10:1–14, 17–30

Jezebel

Queen Jezebel, who helped to make her husband, King Ahab, the most vilified Israelite leader of the Old Testament, is thrown out of a window by her eunuchs, trampled to death by horses, and then eaten by dogs.—II KINGS 9:32–36

Self-righteous people over the centuries have made Jezebel's name a byword for women of questionable morals. But there's no evidence in the Bible that Jezebel had questionable morals. She just didn't have a lot of respect for God.

Jezebel's daughter, while clever enough to become a queen, obviously didn't know much about self-defense.

Jezebel's daughter, Athaliah, rules Judah after having every male heir to the throne murdered. Unfortunately she misses one of her grandsons, and six years later is herself butchered by the followers of the recently resurfaced boy-king.—II KINGS 11:1–16 (also II CHRONICLES 22:10–12; 23:1–15)

The first few chapters of I Chronicles, which are nothing more than genealogical listings, make for THE most tedious reading in the Bible. "Meshobab, Jamlech, Joshah the son of Amaziah, Joel, Jehu the son of Joshibiah, son of Seraiah, son of Asiel, Elioenai, Jaakobah, Jeshohaiah, Asaiah, Adiel, Jesimiel, Benaiah, Ziza the son of Shiphi, son of Allon, son of Jedaiah, son of Shimri, son of Shemaiah. . . ." You get the idea.

King Amaziah of Judah wants to go to war against the nation of Seir, and he hires a hundred thousand Israelite mercenaries to bolster his army. However, God does not approve of Israel at the moment, and he tells the king to dismiss the Israelites and to write off all of the money he's already paid them. King Amaziah obeys. While he's off in Seir, the hundred thousand Israelites return to Judah, sack its cities, and kill three thousand innocent people.—II CHRONICLES 25:5–13

Headstrong King Uzziah, Amaziah's son, enters the temple of the ark of God to burn incense on its altar—an honor reserved for priests. Before Uzziah can even reach the altar, God turns him into a leper.—II CHRONICLES 26:16–21

Angels in the Bible are more often sword-wielding mass murderers than harp-playing messengers of glad tidings. The champion killer is an unnamed angel who, after entering a camp of Assyrians that are besieging Jerusalem, single-handedly slaughters 185,000 of them.—II KINGS 19:35

King Manasseh, great-great grandson of Uzziah, sacrifices his sons to other gods, consorts with mediums and wizards, and sets up graven images in the temple of the ark. God grumbles that He will "wipe Jerusalem as one wipes a dish."—II KINGS 21:1–13

PROMISED LAND POSTSCRIPT

As the books of **Ezra**, **Nehemiah**, and **Esther** begin, the once-mighty nation of Israel has nearly been "wiped" off the face of the earth. Israel, the country, has been conquered and its people carried away by the Assyrians. Judah has been conquered and Jerusalem destroyed by the Babylonians. The temple of the ark of God has been burned and destroyed (as well as the ark itself, to no one's recorded sorrow). A few ragged survivors carry on in Jerusalem and Judea (the former Judah), but they are a feeble minority among the outsiders who now, once again, inhabit the Promised Land.

First appearance in the Bible of the word "Jew."—EZRA 4:12

Nehemiah, governor of Judea, punishes Jewish men who have married non-Jewish women by pulling their hair out. —NEHEMIAH 13:23–25

King Ahasuerus (or, in some Bibles, King Xerxes) orders that every remaining Jew in the world is to be killed. Esther, his queen, reveals that she is a Jew and begs the king to revoke his order. The king refuses (kings, like God, can never admit that they're wrong) but he does issue a second order authorizing the Jews to attack first. "So the Jews struck down all their enemies with the sword, slaughtering and destroying them, and did as they pleased to those who hated them." —ESTHER 3:8–11; 8:3–8, 11; 9:1–6

FROM THE RIDICULOUS
TO THE SUBLIME

The end of the book of Esther marks the end of the chronological historical books of the Old Testament. The next five books are philosophic and poetic and help to reveal the Bible for what it truly is: not *a* book, but a *collection* of books, many having little or nothing to do with their neighbors. Scholars have arranged them, over the centuries, into a ragged kind of order, but from here on it makes for lumpy reading.

The book of **Job** tells the story of Job, the most blameless and upright man on earth, according to God. Troublemaker Satan, however, has a different opinion: he thinks that Job wouldn't be so blameless if his life weren't so pleasant. God can't stand a smug Satan, so He tests Job's faith by destroying his life: He kills his ten children, takes away (or kills) his herds, and covers him with "loathsome sores" from head to toe.

This is good, in a way, as it motivates Job to spend many of the next twenty-nine chapters of his book uttering the most bitter, cynical, and devastating damnations of God to be found in the Bible:

"[God] destroys both the blameless and the wicked. When a scourge brings sudden death, He mocks the despair of the innocent. When a land falls into the hands of the wicked, He blindfolds its judges. If it is not He, then who is it?"—Job 9:22–24

"From the city the dying groan, and the throat of the wounded cries for help; yet God pays no attention to their prayer."—Job 24:12

"Why do the wicked live on, growing old and increasing in power? Their homes are safe . . . their little ones dance . . . they spend their years in prosperity and go down to the grave in peace. It is said, 'God stores up a man's punishments for his sons.' Let Him repay the man himself, so that he will know it!"—Job 21:7–21

Job, far from remaining faithful, has become the Old Testament's most eloquent rebel. And perhaps he would have remained so, a thorn in the side of God, had God not come down in a whirlwind and argued His case personally. ("Have you an arm like God, and can you thunder with a voice like His?") Job quickly sees that his judgments were hasty ("I have uttered what I did not understand. . . .") and a pacified God gives Job more animals than he had before, ten new (and more attractive) children, and 140 more years of life. Job and God agree: "The fear of the Lord—that is wisdom." (Job 28:28)

God's diatribe against Job is pretty shallow, a lengthy example of the "God is more powerful than man so how can a man possibly judge God?" argument. It's also kind of scary, in that it deteriorates into babbling descriptions of Behemoth, a land monster, and Leviathan, a fire-breathing sea monster, which have nothing to do with Job's complaints. What draws Job to God's point of view is not what He says, but that He came down to earth to say it. ("My ears had heard of you but now my eyes have seen you. Therefore I despise myself. . . .")

Job asserts that those who are delighted with the beauty of the sun or the moon are unfaithful to God.—Job 31:26–28

The book of **The Psalms** is a collection of hymn lyrics, with themes split fairly evenly between praising God and whining at Him. They were written at different times by different people, which sometimes creates a great gulf in attitude between one and the next. Compare Psalm 145, which describes God as "... gracious and merciful; slow to anger and abounding in steadfast love ... good to all...." with Psalm 144, where God "... trains my hands for war, and my fingers for battle," and "... subdues the peoples under me."

A lot of people know Psalm 23 ("The Lord is my shepherd...."), a genuinely pretty piece of writing, but few know Psalm 44, which damns God for his lack of support, or Psalms 79, 83, and 109, which plead for God's vindictiveness, or Psalm 18, which describes God as a kind of fire-breathing monster, or Psalms 74 and 88, which are just generally depressing.

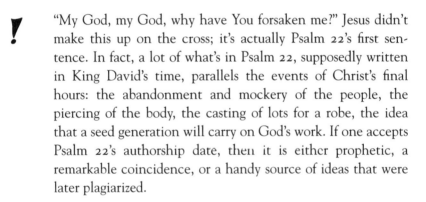

"My God, my God, why have You forsaken me?" Jesus didn't make this up on the cross; it's actually Psalm 22's first sentence. In fact, a lot of what's in Psalm 22, supposedly written in King David's time, parallels the events of Christ's final hours: the abandonment and mockery of the people, the piercing of the body, the casting of lots for a robe, the idea that a seed generation will carry on God's work. If one accepts Psalm 22's authorship date, then it is either prophetic, a remarkable coincidence, or a handy source of ideas that were later plagiarized.

"God will shatter the heads of His enemies, the hairy crown of those who walk in their guilty ways ... that you may bathe your feet in blood, so that the tongues of your dogs may have their share from the foe."—PSALM 68:21, 23

"The Lord is at your right hand; He will shatter kings on the day of His wrath. He will execute judgment among the nations, filling them with corpses...."—PSALM 110:5–6

"Precious in the sight of the Lord is the death of His faithful ones."—PSALM 116:15

Some readers may remember the song "Rivers of Babylon," which was a minor hit a few years back. Its title and lyrics came from the first verse of Psalm 137: "By the rivers of Babylon, there we sat down, yea, we wept, when we remembered Zion."

Its songwriters were more discreet than the original psalmists, who went on to conclude Psalm 137 with these two verses: "O daughter Babylon, you devastator! Happy shall they be who take your little ones and dash them against the rocks!"

The book of **The Proverbs,** which are nuggets of God-approved wisdom, was supposedly written by Solomon. Chapters 5–7 are devoted primarily to decrying the evils of lusty women and of having sex with other men's wives. This discourse comes from the most notorious polygamist in the Bible.

Reading the book of Proverbs is like reading an endless list of Chinese fortune cookie sayings, strung one after another. ("A quarrelsome wife is like a constant dripping on a rainy day," etc.) It is the source of many of the moralist aphorisms quoted by self-righteous Bible-thumpers and self-important rock lyricists. Here are a few proverbs that don't usually get repackaged:

"The mouth of the righteous brings forth wisdom, but a perverse tongue will be cut out."—PROVERBS 10:31

"Like a gold ring in a pig's snout is a beautiful woman who shows no discretion."—PROVERBS 11:22

"The poor are disliked even by their neighbors, but the rich have many friends."—PROVERBS 14:20

"A bribe is a charm to the one who gives it; wherever he turns, he succeeds."—PROVERBS 17:8

"Blows and wounds cleanse away evil, and beatings purge the inmost being."—PROVERBS 20:30

 "Folly is bound up in the heart of a child, but the rod of discipline will drive it far from him."—PROVERBS 22:15

 "Do not withhold discipline from a child. . . . Punish him with the rod, and save his soul from death."—PROVERBS 23:13

"A whip for the horse, a bridle for the donkey, and a rod for the back of fools!"—PROVERBS 26:3

The book of **Ecclesiastes** is an odd one. Written by a nameless, world-weary "Teacher" (supposedly Solomon), it belittles the Proverbs' emphasis on wisdom, at least as it applies to science and theology. Humans can never understand God and His creations, the Teacher tells us; our energies would best be spent keeping quiet, following orders, and blindly accepting our class and situation, no matter how miserable. Life is "meaningless, a chasing after the wind," the Teacher sighs, over and over. "There is nothing better for a man than to enjoy his work, because that is his lot." Other observations by this seriously depressed writer:

"All things are wearisome . . . what has been done will be done again . . . even those who are yet to come will not be remembered by those who follow."—ECCLESIASTES 1:8–11

"...with much wisdom comes much sorrow; the more knowledge, the more grief."—ECCLESIASTES 1:18

"The wise man has eyes in his head while the fool walks in darkness; but...the same fate overtakes them both."—ECCLESIASTES 2:14

"Man's fate is like that of the animals; the same fate awaits them both: As one dies, so dies the other. All have the same breath; man has no advantage over the animal. Everything is meaningless."—ECCLESIASTES 3:19

"It is better to go to a house of mourning than to go to a house of feasting, for death is the destiny of every man.... Sorrow is better than laughter, because a sad face is good for the heart."—ECCLESIASTES 7:2–3

"Go, eat your food with gladness, and drink your wine with a joyful heart.... Enjoy life with your wife, whom you love, all the days of this meaningless life that God has given you...all your meaningless days."—ECCLESIASTES 9:7–9

"A feast is made for laughter and wine makes life merry, but money is the answer for everything."—ECCLESIASTES 10:19

The Teacher ends his Gloomy Gus sermon by crying, "Meaningless! Meaningless! Everything is meaningless!" The book of Ecclesiastes, however, doesn't end here. It continues for six more verses, written by an unidentified commentator. He wraps up the Teacher's book, putting a theologically correct spin on it, with a terse, "Fear God and keep his commandments, for this is the whole duty of man."

What **The Song of Songs** is doing among the sacred books of
the Christian and Hebrew religions is a mystery, though an
explanation might be found in its alternate title, The Song of
Solomon. Regardless of its author, religious authorities have
tried very hard to explain away The Song of Songs' erotic
imagery as an allegory for the chaste love between humankind and the Church. Baloney—The Song of Songs is the
kind of stuff you read aloud to your girl to get her in the
mood.

sex "Like an apple tree among the trees of the forest is my lover
among the young men. I delight to sit in his shade, and his
fruit is sweet to my taste."—SONG OF SONGS 2:3

sex "Blow on my garden, that its fragrance may spread abroad. Let
my lover come into his garden, and taste its choice fruits."
—SONG OF SONGS 4:16

sex "How graceful are your feet in sandals, O queenly maiden!
Your rounded thighs are like jewels, the work of a master
hand. Your navel is a rounded bowl that never lacks mixed
wine. Your belly is a heap of wheat, encircled with lilies."
—SONG OF SONGS 7:1–2

sex "How fair and pleasant you are, O loved one, delectable
maiden! You are stately as a palm tree, and your breasts are
like its clusters. I say I will climb the palm tree and lay hold of
its branches. Oh, may your breasts be like the clusters of the
vine, and the scent of your breath like apples, and your kisses
like the best wine that goes down smoothly, gliding over lips
and teeth."—SONG OF SONGS 7:6–9

sex "O that you were like a brother to me, who nursed at my
mother's breast! If I met you outside, I would kiss you . . . I

would lead you and bring you into the house of my mother, and into the chamber of the one who bore me. I would give you spiced wine to drink, the juice of my pomegranates." —SONG OF SONGS 8:1–2

THE PROPHETS

The last seventeen books of the Old Testament are the domain of the prophets, and if you never thought you'd get tired of reading about apocalyptic carnage, you will by the time you finish these books.

The prophets prophesied because most of the people of Israel no longer believed in God. In fact, by the time the prophets hit their full stride, only the tribe of Judah—just one out of the twelve that Moses had led to the Promised Land—had a measurable number of God worshippers. And they were usually a wretched minority.

Most of the prophets lived in the last years of Judah and Jerusalem and most specialized in preaching hellfire and damnation against their listeners. An occasional screwball, such as Ezekiel, Daniel, or Zechariah, lightens the proceedings with nutty visions, but for the most part the prophets are a dreary bunch.

Perhaps the prophets would make better reading today if they had forecast on a wider range of topics, like space travel or the rise of the Nazis. But they didn't.

With the book of **Isaiah** the Bible whisks the reader back into the reign of Uzziah, the God-made leper king of Judah. Isaiah was an egomaniacal crackpot, and his writings are often overblown and disjointed. It's hard to read certain sections of Isaiah (particularly chapter 29) and *not* think of William Shatner doing a dramatic reading, bugging out his eyes.

Isaiah becomes the second person since Moses to see God. Isaiah also describes Him as sitting on a "throne" but, like Micaiah, provides no other useful details.—ISAIAH 6:1–5

 Isaiah prophesies the birth of a boy named Immanuel. He makes no claims that Immanuel will be any sort of Messiah or that he will "ransom captive Israel" (as a well-known hymn would later insist). Far from it: Immanuel's birth marks the imminent destruction of Israel and of Judah's other pesky neighbor, Syria.—ISAIAH 7:1, 14–16

God whistles, the only time He does so in the Bible. Not because He's happy, but to summon ravaging swarms of flies and bees.—ISAIAH 7:18 (Note: In the King James Version of the Bible, God hisses.)

 Isaiah relishes prophecies of death and carnage, so it's fitting that he is the first in the Bible to predict a worldwide apocalypse. "See, the day of the Lord comes, cruel, with wrath and fierce anger, to make the earth a desolation and to destroy its sinners from it. Their infants will be dashed to pieces before their eyes; their houses will be plundered, and their wives ravished."—ISAIAH 13:9, 16

 More of the same: "The Lord is enraged against all the nations, and furious against all their hoards; He has doomed them, has given them over for slaughter. Their slain shall be cast out, and the stench of their corpses shall rise; the mountains shall flow with their blood."—ISAIAH 34:2–3

Isaiah becomes the first person in the Bible to envision the mass resurrection of God-approved dead people.—ISAIAH 26:19 (Note: Daniel is the first to envision the mass resurrection of God-disapproved dead people.—DANIEL 12:2)

God admits that the only reason He saved the chosen people is because He wanted someone to worship Him.—ISAIAH 43:20–21

God for the first time declares His intention to inflict Himself not only on Israel but on all the people of the earth. He then declares that Isaiah is also much too qualified to restrict his work to the Israelites and promises him a promotion to world-wide zealotry.—ISAIAH 45:22–23; 49:6

God compares Himself, albeit backhandedly, to a woman—the only time in the Bible that He does so.—ISAIAH 49:14–15

God proves that Isaiah's bloody prophecies were dead accurate: "But you who forsake the Lord . . . I will destine you to the sword, and all of you shall bow down to the slaughter. . . ."—ISAIAH 65:11–12

The books of **Jeremiah** and **Lamentations** were supposedly written by the prophet Jeremiah, who lived a couple of kings after Isaiah in the final years of Judah and Jerusalem. Lamentations is mercifully short, but Jeremiah wins the Bible Book I'd Least Like To Read Again award. It's repetitive, relentlessly gloomy, and poorly edited; it jumps back and forth in time without warning or explanation; and it's riddled with conflicting references.

Jeremiah is the most unhappy man in the Bible. Since he's the only man in Judah who will listen to God, God constantly complains to him about how Judah's people are unworthy and rants about how He's going to savagely punish them for their faithlessness. God uses Jeremiah as His spokesman, and Jeremiah thus spends most of his adult life delivering messages of doom to audiences that never listen.

God declares that one of His punishments for the people of Judah will be to personally lift their robes up over their heads, thereby exposing their genitals.—JEREMIAH 13:26 (Note: He also orders the same punishment for Nineveh in Nahum 3:5)

Jeremiah protests to God that, as far as Jerusalem is concerned, he has not "desired the fatal day." Then, only two verses later, he cries, "Bring on them the day of disaster; destroy them with double destruction!"—JEREMIAH 17:16, 18

God orders Jeremiah to wear a cattle yoke to dramatize his prophecies. Then Hananiah, another prophet, breaks Jeremiah's yoke to dramatize *his* prophecies. God kills Hananiah.—JEREMIAH 27:2, 12–15; 28:10–11, 15–17

 "A curse on him who is lax in doing the Lord's work! A curse on him who keeps his sword from bloodshed!"—JEREMIAH 48:10

 Chapter 52 of Jeremiah sums up succinctly what God took fifty-one chapters to explain: Jerusalem was successfully besieged and Judah destroyed by the more powerful kingdom of Babylonia. Jeremiah adds, "It was because of the Lord's anger that all this happened to Jerusalem and Judah . . ." but that's just damage control. The text makes it clear that it was Judah's arrogant king, not God's wrath, that brought the chosen people to their destruction.

Ezekiel is yet another calamity-seeing prophet. By this point most Bible readers are understandably weary of more gloom and doom, but Ezekiel has an advantage over Isaiah and Jeremiah. Ezekiel has visions. And not just any visions, but *insane* visions, of God and of winged creatures with four heads and of flying wheels with eyes in their rims. Ezekiel's visions aren't very coherent—but that's because Ezekiel is a *nut*. And that's what makes his book interesting.

"... when the living creatures rose from the earth, the wheels rose ... along with them; for the spirit of the living creatures was in the wheels." This passage, part of Ezekiel's vision at the Chebar River, is cited by flying saucer buffs as proof that space people have been visiting earth since biblical times. If one reads Ezekiel's entire account, however, it is clear that the only space person visiting the Chebar is Mr. E himself. His "wheel within a wheel" is less a scientific observation than it is a whoozy hallucination.—Ezekiel 1:4–21

Ezekiel's vision looks more like a bad rebus than an earthshaking religious experience.

Ezekiel becomes the third person since Moses to see God. His description—of "a figure like that of a man" who resembles "glowing metal" above the waist and "fire" below—isn't much, but it's the best the Bible has to offer.—EZEKIEL 1:26–28; 8:2

 God humiliates Ezekiel even more than Jeremiah: He makes him eat a parchment scroll, shave off his hair and burn it, and then lie on his left side for thirteen months. God orders Ezekiel to eat only bread baked with human dung for those thirteen months, but Ezekiel begs for mercy. God allows him to eat bread baked with cow dung.—EZEKIEL 3:1–2; 4:9, 12, 14–15; 5:1–4

 God reaches down from heaven with a giant hand, grabs Ezekiel by his hair (it had apparently grown back), and carries him from his home to Jerusalem.—EZEKIEL 8:1–3

God decides to spare a few Jews from Jerusalem's impending annihilation, but only because He wants someone to spread firsthand accounts of His bloody vengeance and to confess that they deserved everything that they got.—EZEKIEL 12:16

 In chapter 16 of Ezekiel, God indulges in a lengthy soliloquy that compares His wrath toward Jerusalem with that of a man who has been spurned by an ungrateful woman. "I gave you My solemn oath . . . and you became Mine," God begins, "but you trusted in your beauty. . . . You lavished your favors on anyone who passed by and your beauty became his. You adulterous wife! You prefer strangers to your own Husband! Therefore, you prostitute, hear the word of the Lord! I will hand you over to your lovers . . . who will stone you and hack you to pieces with their swords."—EZEKIEL 16:1–40

 In chapter 23 God drags the Bible completely into the gutter by comparing Israel and Judah to two slutty sisters. After the two bear children for God (like Father, like sons: see Genesis 6), they run off and indulge in a wild orgy of abominable deeds that the Bible describes in lurid detail. Passages such as "[She] played the whore while she was Mine . . . and defiled herself with all the idols . . ." and ". . . men had lain with her and fondled her virgin bosom and poured out their lust upon her," are explicit enough, but this chapter also contains the infamous verse 20, with its references to donkey-sized dicks and horsey semen. The girls, of course, meet bloody ends for their sinful ways (and their children are butchered as well) and God, in a refinement of chapter 16, justifies His savage justice as a moral lesson: "Thus I will put an end to lewdness in the land, so that all women may take warning and not commit lewdness as you have done."—EZEKIEL 23

God confesses that the only reason He didn't kill all of the chosen people while they were in the wilderness is that it would have made Him look bad.—EZEKIEL 20:13–14

God admits that He gave His chosen people purposefully bogus laws and rituals in the wilderness to make their lives miserable.—EZEKIEL 20:25–26

God decrees that no matter how much the chosen people may want God to go away and leave them alone, He will never let them go.—EZEKIEL 20:32–33

God kills Ezekiel's wife and orders him not to mourn her death. In this way, Ezekiel is to set an example of self-tortured behavior that all the Jewish exiles are to follow when they hear that Jerusalem has fallen. The Bible is mum on whether any of Ezekiel's audience goes along.—EZEKIEL 24:15–24

Chapters 26 through 39 of Ezekiel show God in one of His

most murderous moods. He has already overseen the destruction of Judah and Jerusalem, but this apparently hasn't been enough, and in these chapters He luridly outlines His plans for the butchering of Judah's neighboring nations: Moab will become a "horror," the Ammonites will be "burned with fire," the people of Elam will be "consumed."

God's triumphant mantra of revenge, which follows each detailed description of obliteration, is, "Then they shall know that I am the Lord."

 "I will let ... the wild animals of the whole earth gorge themselves with you. I will strew your flesh on the mountains, and fill the valleys with your carcass. I will drench the land with your flowing blood up to the mountains...."—EZEKIEL 32:4–6

God tells Ezekiel that he must never cease serving as God's dreary-news mouthpiece for the Jews, for if he ever does, He will hold Ezekiel accountable for their blood.—EZEKIEL 33:7–9

 God explains his philosophy of damnation and salvation: If you're good and then you go bad, you're damned, but if you're bad and then you do good, you're saved. One might reasonably ask, "What of the good person who goes bad and then repents? Or of the bad person who does good and then backslides?" God, unfortunately, doesn't take His reasoning this far.—EZEKIEL 33:12–20 (also 18:21–29)

 "As I live, surely those who are in the waste places shall fall by the sword; and those who are in the open field I will give to the wild animals to be devoured; and those who are in strongholds and in caves shall die by pestilence.... Then they shall know that I am the Lord, when I have made the land a desolation and a waste...."—EZEKIEL 33:27, 29

God explains that the only reason He's sparing a few survivors among His chosen people is because He would look bad if they all died.—EZEKIEL 36:22–23, 32

God doesn't want anyone near Him who sweats.—EZEKIEL 44:17–18

God warns that holiness can be transferred by clothing. —EZEKIEL 44:19

If Jeremiah was the Bible's Yin, then **Daniel** is its Yang. Jeremiah preached God's word to God's people in God's land and got nothing but grief; Daniel preaches God's word to a heathen king in a hostile land and gets nothing but glory.

The book of Daniel is only twelve chapters long, but those chapters divide neatly into two very different books. The first six chapters contain the stories that every Sunday-school kid knows: Daniel in the lion's den; the mysterious finger writing on the wall; Shadrach, Meshach, and Abednego (yo!); and the exploits of nutty old King Nebuchadnezzar. The second six are more obscure and recount Daniel's murky dreams and visions of the future, weird even by the standards of the Bible. If you thought Ezekiel was a kook, wait till you read Daniel.

Daniel and his pals Shadrach, Meshach, and Abednego refuse to eat King Nebuchadnezzar's rich food and instead subsist on a diet of vegetables. The Bible regards it as something of a minor miracle when, after ten days, the boys from Judah looked healthier and better nourished than those who had pigged out with the king.—DANIEL 1:8–15

King Nebuchadnezzar
With King Nebuchadnezzar, the Bible finally creates a human character as mentally unstable as God. Nebuchadnezzar's

mood swings are astonishing: one minute he threatens to tear his closest advisors into pieces, the next he falls on his face before crazy Daniel, showering him with gifts and honors. One wonders how he ever became, as the Bible insists, the most powerful ruler of his time.

Nebuchadnezzar erects a gold statue ninety feet tall and orders all of his subordinates to worship it. Shadrach, Meshach, and Abednego, now bureaucratic officials in Babylon, refuse, and the easily enraged king orders that all three be thrown into a furnace. The furnace is so hot that it kills the men who toss Shadrach, Meshach, and Abednego into it (another example of King N's questionable style of governing), yet all three emerge completely unharmed. Nebuchadnezzar is so impressed that he gives Shadrach, Meshach, and Abednego promotions, but the Bible makes no mention of Nebuchadnezzar taking down his statue.—DANIEL 3

An angel shields Daniel's friends with asbestos wings while fire consumes those who are idolatrous and unimportant.

God finally tires of King Nebuchadnezzar's cockiness, so He turns the king into a madman. "He was driven away from human society, ate grass like oxen ... his hair grew as long as eagles' feathers and his nails became like birds' claws." —DANIEL 4:29–33

For all the good Bible press that Daniel has enjoyed over the years (Ezekiel views him as a spiritual equal of Noah and Job), he is curiously noncommittal: more a mystic than a zealot. Yes, Daniel stood up for God when the Babylonians used His temple vessels as tableware (this event triggered the spooky "handwriting on the wall" incident), but he also served voluntarily in Nebuchadnezzar's court, was sincere when he called him "my lord" and "the king of kings," and never expressed any anger over his destruction of Jerusalem or Judah. Remember: it was Shadrach, Meshach, and Abednego who risked the furnace; Daniel was conspicuously absent.

You probably know the story of Daniel in the lion's den: how he was condemned to spend a night in it because he prayed to God, and how an angel shut the lions' mouths so that Daniel could emerge the next morning unscathed. What you probably don't know is that immediately after Daniel was pulled out, all of Daniel's accusers were thrown in—along with all their wives and children—and mauled to death. —DANIEL 6:24

The most curious thing about the book of Daniel is its polytheistic attitude toward God; its pages repeatedly refer to Him as "the God of heaven," "a great God," "our God," even "the God of gods." None of these monikers appears earlier in the Bible, and all gently sidestep the endorsement of an all-purpose deity. God may be the best, the book of Daniel seems to say, but He is not alone.

The Daniel who totters along in chapters 7–12 of his book is a bona fide nutcake; a seer haunted by visions; a man who receives messages from a creature with flaming eyes that floats above the Tigris River. What does Daniel's "beast with teeth of iron" symbolize? When are the "latter days" and who is the "prince of princes"? Is Daniel ranting about Jesus and the Devil and the end of the world—or about some local boundary dispute that faded from memory twenty-five hundred years ago?

Daniel's ravings are just the kind of material that religious wackos relish; they sound so ominous and important that they should mean *something*, yet they're so opaque and muddled that they could mean anything. They will never lack for interpreters; someone will always be around, earnest, eager, and self-assured, to explain them.

 The only appearance of the word "intelligence" in the Bible is in Daniel, and only in the archaic English of the King James Version. It means "favorable regard." It has been revised out of every modern translation.—DANIEL 11:30

 With **Hosea**, the Bible returns to the times of Isaiah and once again fills page after page with gloomy prophecies and repetitive, heavy-handed allegory. Hosea, however, is a relatively fortunate prophet in that God orders him to dramatize his predictions by having sex. Kids result from these dalliances, and God gives them funny names (such as "Not Loved" and "Not My People") in His quest for a good religious metaphor.

 God compares Himself to mildew and to a bug.—HOSEA 5:12

The Bible never reveals what happens to the kids that God ordered Hosea to sire. But considering what *did* happen to their country and to their neighbors—events that Hosea luridly describes in his prophecies—it probably wasn't pleasant. "They shall fall by the sword; their little ones shall be dashed in pieces, and their pregnant women ripped open."—Hosea 13:16

Joel is yet another prophet of doom. "Let all the inhabitants of the land tremble, for the day of the Lord is coming. It is near. . . ." Since Joel has nothing original to offer, one can safely avoid reading his book.

Amos is noteworthy only in that his book is so typical of the doomsayers. It's 146 verses long and breaks down as follows: one establishes background, five offer a glimpse of a distant, rosy future, and the 140 in between deliver nonstop nagging, judgment, and calamity.

God speaks to the people of Israel as the unforgiving father that He is: "You only have I chosen of all the families of the earth; therefore I will punish you for all your sins."—Amos 3:2

Amos enthusiastically brags of God's power: "When disaster comes to a city, has not the Lord caused it?"—Amos 3:6

God reviews a laundry list of horrors that He's recently unloaded on the people of Israel—famine, drought, crop blight, insect infestations, war—and after each example He damns them because they "did not return to Me." One might reasonably ask, Isn't this the same God who rained plagues on Egypt so that it would expel the Israelites? Why is He so shocked that His miserable people have expelled Him? No matter: ". . . prepare to meet your God, O Israel!"—Amos 4:6–12

A priest warns Amos not to prophesy any more in Israel. Amos, as tactful as any Bible zealot, tells the priest: ". . . thus says the Lord: 'Your wife shall become a prostitute ... your sons and your daughters shall fall by the sword ... you yourself shall die in an unclean land. ...'"—AMOS 7:17

Obadiah is the most enjoyable Old Testament prophet to read. His book is only twenty-one verses long.

One can't help but admire **Jonah**, the only Old Testament prophet smart enough to run for the hills as soon as God starts ordering him around. True, he doesn't escape, but at least he doesn't end up with a dead wife like Ezekiel, or forced to walk around wearing a cattle yoke like Jeremiah.

 Jonah, trapped on a stormy sea by God, is thrown overboard by his fearful shipmates. He is promptly swallowed by a "great fish" (the Bible never uses the word "whale") in which God lets him partially digest for three days. Only when God is firmly convinced that Jonah has recanted his rebellious ways does He order the fish to vomit him up.—JONAH 1:3–17; 2:10

Jonah was a complex man. But we hate complexity in Bible stories, so he's been reduced to equal billing with a dyspeptic fish.

Micah's saving grace among the doomsayers is his histrionic hyperbole. His writings have a flair that goes beyond the usual prophetic spleen. William Shatner (see Isaiah) was born to narrate the audio cassette of this book.

Some praise Micah for his "act justly and love mercy" definition of religious fundamentals (6:8), some for being the first to foretell of a Messiah from Bethlehem (5:2), but honestly, these people are being very selective. Micah is a ranting lunatic who best reveals himself (and his fellow prophets) with his pledge to "...weep and wail...go about barefoot and naked...howl like a jackal and moan like an owl." (1:8)

Nahum's specialty is prophesying the impending destruction of Nineveh, the capital of Hebrew-harrassing Assyria. He does so with gusto:

"Woe to the city of blood, full of lies, full of plunder, never without victims!...piles of dead, bodies without number, people stumbling over the corpses...."—NAHUM 3:1–3

"The river gates are thrown open and the palace collapses.... Its slave girls moan... and beat upon their breasts.... 'Stop! Stop!' they cry, but no one turns back. Plunder the silver! Plunder the gold! The supply is endless, the wealth from all its treasures! She is pillaged, plundered, stripped!"—NAHUM 2:6–10

Habakkuk spends ten of his fifty-six verses complaining to God, and most of what's left listening to God's answers.

God obsesses on nudity once again: "Woe to him who gives drink to his neighbors, pouring it from the wineskin till they are drunk, so that he can gaze on their naked bodies. You will be filled with shame instead of glory. Now it is your turn! Drink and be exposed!"—HABAKKUK 2:15–16

God damns Judah for "the violence you have done" and "your destruction of animals." He is shocked that "... you have shed man's blood; you have destroyed lands and cities and everyone in them." God has apparently forgotten Who it was that ordered King Saul to destroy the cities of the Amalekites and to butcher every last soul, and animal, in them.— HABAKKUK 2:17 (see I SAMUEL 15:2–3)

Zephaniah spends his three chapters reciting the usual litany of gloom and destruction. But he *is* a little different in that he describes a God so eager for blood that He would violate His "never again will I destroy all living creatures" covenant with Noah (GENESIS 8:21). As if God violating His covenants would be anything new.

 "I will utterly sweep away everything ... I will sweep away humans and animals; I will sweep away the birds of the air and the fish of the sea . . . I will cut off humanity from the face of the earth."—ZEPHANIAH 1:2–3

 "That day will be a day of wrath ... I will bring distress upon people ... their blood shall be poured out like dust, and their flesh like dung."—ZEPHANIAH 1:15–17

 "... in the fire of His passion the whole earth shall be consumed, for a full, terrible end He will make of all the inhabitants of the earth."—ZEPHANIAH 1:18

Haggai doesn't concern himself with the apocalypse. He's a contemporary of Nehemiah, and the sole purpose of his prophecy is to get the surviving Jews in Jerusalem off of their butts and into the rebuilding of God's destroyed temple.

The God of Haggai motivates by subtle fear rather than by fire-and-brimstone damnation. He constantly exhorts his audiences to "give careful thought" to their actions—while hinting that the drought and crop failures that they're suffering might miraculously end once His temple is rebuilt.

Haggai wasn't much of a prophet. He ends his book by heaping praise on Zerubbabel, the governor of Judea, and declaring that God will "make you like a signet ring, for I have chosen you." Chosen for what is unclear, and after a few more mentions Zerubbabel disappears from the Bible, never having been chosen for anything.

Zechariah is another prophet who has visions, some of which are worthy of note, including one of a thirty-foot-long flying scroll that destroys the houses of thieves (5:1–4) and another of two women with "wings like the wings of a stork" who fly around with Wickedness—another woman— in a basket (5:6–11).

To everyone's relief, the God of Zechariah actually seems mellow, His wrath apparently, thankfully, spent. "Love truth and peace," He purrs to the Jews who struggle to survive in the country that He helped to destroy. "I have purposed in these days to do good to Jerusalem and to the house of Judah; do not be afraid."

If the God of Zechariah is not as angry with the people of Judah as He was in the past, He is much angrier with a surprising new irritant: the prophets themselves.

God foresees a day when He will outlaw prophesy among His people. "And if anyone still prophesies, his father and mother, to whom he was born, will say to him, 'You must die because you have told lies in the Lord's name.' When he prophesies his own parents will stab him."—ZECHARIAH 13:2–3

The outlawing of the prophets provides insight into Bible-era friendships: "On that day every prophet will be ashamed of his prophetic vision. If someone asks him, 'What are these wounds on your body?' he will answer, 'The wounds I was given at the house of my friends.'"—ZECHARIAH 13:4, 6

 Despite his role as an antiprophet mouthpiece, Zechariah is one himself, and as such he can't resist a little doom saying: "This shall be the plague with which the Lord will strike all the peoples that wage war against Jerusalem: Their flesh shall rot while they are still on their feet, their eyes shall rot in their sockets, and their tongues shall rot in their mouths." —ZECHARIAH 14:12

Malachi paints a picture of God as a kind of cranky old coot: blunt and with no tolerance for flowery prose.

God threatens to smear animal dung on the faces of Israelite priests who don't toe the line.—MALACHI 2:1–3

 "I hate divorce," God snorts. Not on moral grounds, but because it deprives Him of "godly offspring."—MALACHI 2:15–16

 God compares Himself to laundry soap.—MALACHI 3:2

"... I will send you the prophet Elijah before the great and dreadful day of the Lord comes," God promises, "... or else I will come and strike the land with a curse."—MALACHI 4:5–6

With these uncomforting words, leaving the reader with two miserable options, the Old Testament ends.

Welcome to

THE NEW TESTAMENT

As God is the star of the Old Testament, so Jesus is the star of the New. The **New Testament** is made up of twenty-seven books: the first five are historical; the next twenty-one, which are letters written by early Christians, discuss theology; and the last book is prophetic.

The shift from Old Testament to the New is akin to shifting from first gear directly into overdrive. Gone are the droning, endless repetitions of the same names, events, and themes of the prophets; gone, too, are their murky, inscrutable allegory and metaphor. In its place is the story of Jesus, well written in clean, snappy prose that *moves*. Jesus can't help but shine when compared to his wretched Old Testament lead-ins.

THE FOUR GOSPELS

The story of Jesus is told four times in the first four books of the New Testament, written by Matthew, Mark, Luke, and

John. Their accounts of Jesus' life and teachings are called the "Gospels," a word derived from the Anglo-Saxon "godspell" or "good story." It's natural to assume that Matthew, Mark, Luke, and John were four of Jesus' twelve disciples, but that's only half-true: Matthew and John were, Mark and Luke were not.

Mark's account is the shortest and the most direct. John's account, peppered as it is with repeated references to "the disciple whom Jesus loved" (guess who), which are not found in any other Gospel, is the most suspect.

¡JESUS SI! ¡MESSIAH NO!

 It's clear from reading the Gospels that Jesus was not the Messiah prophesied in the Old Testament.

This is not to deny that Jesus had a lot of good things to say or that he worked miracles of healing; all the Gospels agree that he did. But he was not the Messiah prophesied in the Old Testament, and every attempt in the Gospels to prove that he is, through citing Old Testament scripture, is laughable.

Judaic dogma during Jesus' lifetime stipulated that a Messiah meet two fundamental requirements: 1) he had to be a descendent of King David, and 2) he had to be born in Bethlehem. (A third, that he had to be male, went without question.) The two Gospels that try to fit Jesus into this mold both fail miserably. They don't even agree with each other, offering radically different accounts of Jesus' genealogy and his early years.

One doesn't need to check Matthew and Luke against their cited scriptures to see the futility of their effort. One need only observe the actions of the Jewish nationalists and zealots who followed Jesus. To them, the Messiah was to be a warrior, a bloody king of revenge who would lead the Jews in triumph and slaughter over their oppressors—and the reason that they believed this is because that's how the Messiah was described by the prophets of the Old Testament. When Jesus turned out not to meet those expectations—to be a story-teller, not a street fighter—the nationalists and zealots felt betrayed and angered. "Crucify him!" they cried at his trial.

Why did Jesus string these extremists along, eventually ensuring their hatred? Why didn't he just admit that he wasn't the Messiah? Perhaps he felt that his message of moral rebellion only stood a chance of acceptance in Judea's polit-ical tinderbox if he had the extremists on his side. And, too, it's clear from the Gospels that he gradually came to believe that he was what his followers said he was. His own eventual inability to deny his Messiahhood publicly gave his enemies the smoking gun they needed to destroy him. All his teach-ings to the contrary, Jesus was a victim of his own ego.

The need to believe that Jesus was the Messiah prophe-sied in the Old Testament has long passed, and one would have hoped that this would have freed his teachings from reli-gious shackles. Unfortunately, they have been shackled and reshackled again by a new need to believe—that Jesus was the Son of God.

It's sad that people today take the mythical hoodoo spun around Jesus as fact and defend it passionately while ignoring his teachings of universal humility, compassion, and brotherhood.

WHY JESUS IS BETTER THAN GOD

The Message

Since the days of Moses, the way to be true to God was to observe a strict set of rules: certain foods couldn't be eaten, certain sacrifices had to be made, the sabbath had to be com-pletely devoid of any labor, etc. It was all very straightforward and businesslike: the core of the "deal" between God and His chosen people.

Jesus challenged this way of thinking. God's commandments, he preached, did not constitute a soulless contract that could be honored simply by mechanically following rituals. They were a mandate for ethical behavior.

God's blessings couldn't be bought with rich temple contributions, and God wasn't impressed with strict adherence to arcane rites. Jesus declared that what pleased God were good deeds and a good attitude and—this was the kicker—that God rewarded those who pleased Him with eternal life in paradise! This new view of God had enormous appeal to the downtrodden and to the powerless. It gave them hope that, despite their earthly disadvantages, they had a chance at a heavenly prize.

The Delivery

Jesus taught in parables, folksy stories that sound mundane but that actually disguise deep moral truths. The contrast between the apparent and the real message makes a good parable a powerful aid to learning, and Jesus was a genius at creating good parables.

Understanding a parable usually requires effort by the listener (which makes learning active and personal) and the help of a teacher (which ensures that the message delivered is the message received). Parables shine in comparison to the murky metaphors and allegories of the prophets and the thunderous Old Testament pronouncements of God.

Jesus didn't bother to explain most of his parables to the crowds that he addressed. Consequently, most of the people who heard Jesus' parables didn't understand them. He wanted it that way: being indirect protected him from his enemies.

The ultimate genius of the Gospels—and the reason that Jesus' teaching still packs a wallop after two millennia—is that we as readers are allowed backstage. We are privy not only to Jesus' clever words, but to his explanation of them. We become one of his disciples.

The Image
The final triumph of Jesus is packaging. A god without an image may work for a religion restricted to a chosen people, but it won't wash for a religion that seeks nothing less than the voluntary hug of the entire world.

Who are prospective converts more likely to embrace: a god (like God) who won't let them see His face, who will strike them dead on a whim, whose basic demand is that they fear Him—or a nice young man?

THE STORY OF JESUS

Christian fundamentalists portray Jesus as a street-corner evangelist continually exhorting his followers to be "born again" (JOHN 3:3). Established churches portray him as the warm and fuzzy bringer of "good news" (MARK 1:14–15). Both ignore the Jesus that damned both organized religion and the family and that preached the establishment of a pacifist, communist world-state.

It may surprise some that the story of Jesus—which *is* the Bible to many American Christians—takes up only ninety-three pages in a Bible that is 923 pages long.

Part One: The Early Years
The story of Jesus' early life moves along at such a clip that one becomes immediately suspicious: events that would have merited a chapter, or at least a lengthy paragraph, in the Old Testament are dismissed in Matthew and Luke (the only two Gospels that tackle it) in a few words or a sentence. One may well ask, If Jesus was so important and if the Gospels were written so soon after his death, how come the details are so skimpy?

The angel Gabriel tells the virgin Mary how she is to be impregnated: "The Holy Spirit will come upon you, and the power of the Most High will overshadow you."—LUKE 1:35

The virgin birth of Jesus should not be confused with the Immaculate Conception of Mary, though many people do. The Immaculate Conception is the belief that *Mary* was conceived without the "original sin" of Eve, a stigma every other woman must bear. This belief does not appear anywhere in the Bible, and in fact was concocted by Bernard of Clairvaux in the very unbiblical twelfth century.

Joseph wants a divorce after he finds out that Mary is pregnant. God has to send an angel to talk him out of it.—MATTHEW 1:18–24

The Bible never states, anywhere, that Jesus was born on December 25. Nor does it state anywhere that he rose from the dead the first Sunday after the full moon that occurs on or next after March 21, which is how the Easter holiday is determined.

Unlike the well-known Christmastime hymn, the Bible never calls the wise men who came to visit Jesus "kings," and it never says how many there were. There could have been three—or two, or ten, or fifty.—MATTHEW 2:1–2, 7–12

It's clear from the Gospel of Matthew that Jesus wasn't a new-born baby when the wise men came to visit. He was probably around two years old, and he was living in a house. (MATTHEW 2:1–2, 7–12, 16) It was the *shepherds* who visited baby Jesus in the manger.—LUKE 2:8–13

God engineers the removal of infant Jesus from Herod's domain. This results in the slaughter of untold numbers of

Peek-a-boo, I see you! Bethlehem's babies are brutally butchered, but it's okay because they are godless.

innocent children, but the Bible passes over this without comment.—MATTHEW 2:16

John the Baptist sees "... the Spirit descending from heaven like a dove ..." when Jesus is baptized (JOHN 1:32–34). This vision, when attributed to a man who wears camel skins, lives in a desert, and eats only grasshoppers and wild honey, loses a lot of its credibility—which is perhaps why the other three Gospels have Jesus see the Spirit and John keep his mouth shut.

Part Two: Mid-Life Crises

It doesn't take Jesus long to begin preaching something very different from Judaic dogma. "Love your enemies and pray for those who persecute you," he commands. "Be perfect . . . as your heavenly Father is perfect." (MATTHEW 5:43–48) When did the God of the Old Testament ever love His enemies? And when did He ever express a desire for humankind to be anything more than a groveling worship machine?

COMMIE JESUS

"You cannot serve both God and money."—MATTHEW 6:24; LUKE 16:13

". . . it is easier for a camel to go through the eye of a needle than for someone who is rich to enter the kingdom of God."—MATTHEW 19:24; MARK 10:25; LUKE 18:25

". . . woe to you who are rich, for you have already received your comfort."—LUKE 6:24

"Be on your guard against all kinds of greed; for one's life does not consist in the abundance of possessions."—LUKE 12:15

"Sell all that you own and distribute the money to the poor, and you will have treasure in heaven."—LUKE 18:22; MARK 10:21; MATTHEW 19:21

"What is highly valued among men is detestable in God's sight."—LUKE 16:15

ILL-FAVORED INCIDENTS

"...[Jesus] came to a village where a woman named Martha opened her home to him. She had a sister called Mary, who sat at the Lord's feet listening to what he said. But Martha was distracted by all the preparations that had to be made. She came to him and asked, 'Lord, don't you care that my sister has left me to do the work by myself? Tell her to help me!'

"'Martha, Martha,' the Lord answered. 'You are worried and upset about many things, but only one thing is needed. Mary has chosen what is better....'"—LUKE 10:38–42

Jesus forgives the sins of a nameless prostitute, but only after she wets his feet with her tears, wipes them with her hair, pours perfume on them, and kisses them.—LUKE 7:44–48

Nowhere in the Bible is it ever suggested that Mary Magdalene is a prostitute, or that Jesus ever had sex with her, or with anyone.—LUKE 8:1–3

A Samaritan town does not welcome the arrival of Jesus. James and John, two of his disciples, want to be helpful. "Lord, do you want us to command fire to come down from heaven and consume them?"—LUKE 9:51–55

TUBBY JESUS

Jesus may have been fat. The Gospels often depict him as eating and encouraging others to do likewise, and he always complains when people are bothered by it:

He rebuffs John the Baptist's disciples when they gripe about his well-fed followers.—MATTHEW 9:14–15; MARK 2:18–19; LUKE 5:33–34

Tubby Jesus turns his eyes toward heaven and his hands toward a dinner roll. Perhaps he's offering thanks for flowing robes.

He complains to a Galilee crowd that, "[I] came eating and drinking, and you say, 'Look, a glutton and a drunkard...'"
—MATTHEW 11:19; LUKE 7:34

He proclaims himself to be "Lord of the Sabbath" so that he and his disciples can gather food whenever they want.—MATTHEW 12:1–8; MARK 2:23–28; LUKE 6:1–5

When tubby Jesus is hungry, he becomes dangerously cranky. "In the morning, when [Jesus] returned to the city, he was hungry. And seeing a fig tree by the side of the road, he went up to it and found nothing at all on it except leaves. Then he said to it, 'May no fruit ever come from you again!' And the fig tree withered at once."—MATTHEW 21:18–19; MARK 11:12–14, 20–22

Jesus gets mad at the people of certain cities because, despite his miracle working, they haven't repented. ". . . I tell you that on the day of judgment it will be more tolerable for the land of Sodom than for you."—MATTHEW 11:20–24; LUKE 10:10–12

John the Baptist is beheaded by King Herod. The woman-blaming Gospels note that the king "was deeply grieved" and places the blame squarely on the shoulders of Herod's tramp niece and her scheming mother.—MARK 6:17–29; MATTHEW 14:3–11

The Bible never claims that the niece who danced to remove John the Baptist's head was named Salome. In fact, the Bible doesn't name her at all.

Jesus, sulking, refuses to perform miracles in his home town of Nazareth because its residents don't "honor" him.—MATTHEW 13:54–58

Luke's version of the above incident adds that Jesus told the people of Nazareth that none of them were worthy of his message. The people of Nazareth respond by trying to throw him off of a cliff.—LUKE 4:24–29

When Peter, Jesus' most faithful disciple, disagrees with him, Jesus accuses him of being a mouthpiece for Satan.—MATTHEW 16:21–23; MARK 8:32–33

Jesus refuses to heal the demon-possessed child of a Canaanite woman, explaining, "It is not fair to take the children's food and throw it to the dogs." The woman kneels before Jesus and meekly pleads that the "children" (of God) are her "masters." Jesus responds, "For saying that, you may go—the demon has left your daughter."—MARK 7:24–30; MATTHEW 15:21–28

DUM-DUM DISCIPLES

When reading the Gospels, one wonders why Jesus, who taught in parables, picked such dopes to be his disciples:

". . . Jesus said to them, 'Don't you understand this parable? How then will you understand any parable?' "—MARK 4:13

"After he had left the crowd and entered the house, his disciples asked him about this parable. 'Are you so dull?' he asked."—MARK 7:17–18

"As they were coming down the mountain, Jesus gave them orders not to tell anyone what they had seen until the Son of Man had risen from the dead. They kept the matter to themselves, discussing what 'rising from the dead' meant."—MARK 9:9–10

The confusion of Jesus' disciples is sometimes understandable. As the Last Supper nears, he tells them, "You will be betrayed even by parents . . . and they will put some of you to death." Then, only one verse later, he declares, "But not a hair of your head will perish."—LUKE 21:16, 18

James is the only disciple whose fate is mentioned in the Bible. He is, of course, brutally murdered.—ACTS 12:1–2

Jesus predicts that some of his disciples will still be alive when judgment day arrives. (MATTHEW 16:27–28, MARK 9:1, LUKE 9:27) He embellishes on this by proclaiming, "At that time men will see the Son of Man coming in clouds with great power and glory. And he will send his angels and gather his elect from... the ends of the earth to the ends of the heavens. I tell you the truth, this generation will certainly not pass away until all these things have happened." (MARK 13:26–30; MATTHEW 24:30–34; LUKE 21:27–32)

Jesus spoke of "false messiahs and false prophets" who would precede judgment day (MATTHEW 24:24; MARK 13:22), but never of a single antichrist. The apostle Paul created that concept (II THESSALONIANS 2:3), while credit for the catchy name goes to the apostle John (I JOHN 2:18).

THE ARROGANT LAMB

"Do not think that I have come to bring peace to the earth; I have not come to bring peace, but a sword."—MATTHEW 10:34; LUKE 12:49–51

"... none of you can become my disciple if you do not give up all your possessions."—LUKE 14:33

Jesus is approached by a man whose little boy is possessed by a demon. "'... If you can do anything,'" the boy's father cries, "'take pity on us and help us.' 'If you can?'" Jesus replies. —MARK 9:22–23

"You faithless generation, how much longer must I be among you? How much longer must I put up with you?"—MARK 9:19

Jesus forbids his followers from calling anyone on earth "father" or "teacher." These names are to be reserved expressly for God and you-know-who.—MATTHEW 23:9–10

Jesus allows an unidentified woman to pour a jar of very expensive perfume over his head as he reclines at a dinner table (again with the eating...). The disciples are upset at this waste; wouldn't it have been better to sell the perfume and distribute the money to the poor? Jesus responds, "... you will always have the poor with you, but you will not always have me."—MATTHEW 26:6–11; MARK 14:3–7; JOHN 12:2–8

Few consider that when Jesus proclaims, "I am the good shepherd; I know my sheep and my sheep know me..." that he's comparing his followers to one of the stupidest animals in zoology.—JOHN 10:14

JESUS TALKS ABOUT THE FAMILY

"...I have come to set a man against his father, and a daughter against her mother, and a daughter-in-law against her mother-in-law; and one's foes will be members of one's own household."—MATTHEW 10:35–36; LUKE 12:52–53

Could Jesus have had a button nose and a clean shave?
These pixieish Israelites say, "What's so strange about that?"

"Whoever loves father or mother more than me is not worthy of me; and whoever loves son or daughter more than me is not worthy of me. . . ."—MATTHEW 10:37

"Whoever comes to me and does not hate father and mother, wife and children, brothers and sisters . . . cannot be my disciple."—LUKE 14:26

"Now when Jesus saw great crowds around him, he gave orders to go over to the other side [of the lake]. . . . [A] disciple said to him, 'Lord, first let me go and bury my father.' But Jesus said to him, 'Follow me, and let the dead bury their own dead.'"—MATTHEW 8:18, 21–22

"Another [disciple] said, 'I will follow you, Lord; but let me first say farewell to those at home.' Jesus said to him, 'No one who puts a hand to the plow and looks back is fit for the Kingdom of God.'"—LUKE 9:61–62

"As Jesus was saying these things a woman in the crowd called out, 'Blessed is the mother who gave you birth and nursed you.' He replied, 'Blessed rather are those who hear the word of God and obey it.'"—LUKE 11:27–28

"While [Jesus] was still speaking to the crowds, his mother and his brothers were outside, wanting to speak to him. Someone told him, 'Look, your mother and your brothers are standing outside, wanting to speak to you.' . . . Jesus replied, 'Who is my mother, and who are my brothers?' And pointing to his disciples, he said, 'Here are my mother and my brothers!'"—MATTHEW 12:46–49; LUKE 8:19–21

Mark includes a detail in the above story that Matthew and Luke omit: Jesus' mother and brothers made their visit, ". . . to restrain him, for people were saying, 'He has gone out of his mind.' "—MARK 3:21

A GOSPELFUL OF MIRACLES

 Only one miracle performed by Jesus appears in all four Gospels: the feeding of five thousand people with five loaves of bread. While this certainly was no cheap trick, it still smacks of slight-of-hand magic. The Gospels skip over the actual "miracle moment" and provide no clue as to how it was manifest: no references to loaves duplicating themselves or to growing new ends when the old ones are broken off. "Jesus then took the [five] loaves, gave thanks, and distributed to those who were seated as much as they wanted," reads the Gospel of John. The next sentence, which one would hope would provide some detail, instead reads, "When they had all had enough to eat. . . ."—JOHN 6:11–12

On the other hand, the Bible ascribes a full fourteen miracles to Jesus that appear in only one Gospel and not in any of the others. In contrast to the murky five-loaves episode, these miracles are mostly vivid, in-your-face, and visually undisputable; they include raising the dead, instantly healing lepers, making the blind from birth see, and magically restoring a severed ear.

 The miracle in which Jesus changes water into wine is a one-Gospel wonder, and the only person who actually tastes the transmutation is the manager of a wedding banquet who's been drinking all day.—JOHN 2:1–10

 The water-into-wine miracle is precipitated by a comment from Mary to her son: "They have no more wine." Jesus' languid reply is, "Dear woman, why do you involve me?"—JOHN 2:3–4

Jesus uses his divine powers to expel a minor lizard demon.
Today we use Librium but we don't build a religion around it.

Jesus yells at some demons that are infesting a crazy man. The demons fly into a herd of two thousand pigs who then rush into a lake and drown themselves. The pigs' shepherds run off and tell their friends what's happened. The people then come out to meet Jesus—to beg him to please go away.—MARK 5:1–17; LUKE 8:26–37; MATTHEW 8:28–34

Jesus is a miracle battery; merely touching his cloak discharges him, and he can feel it when his healing powers are drained.—MARK 5:24–30; LUKE 8:43–46

Jesus heals with his spit.—MARK 7:33; 8:23; JOHN 9:6–7

Jesus, who plans to raise Lazarus from the dead, orders the stone rolled back from the front of his tomb. Lazarus' sister, unaware of Jesus' intent, is horrified. "Lord," she reminds Jesus, "by this time there is a bad odor, for he has been in there four days."—JOHN 11:38–39

HELLFIRE JESUS

"I tell you, on the day of judgment you will have to give an account for every careless word you utter; for by your words you will be justified, and by your words you will be condemned."—MATTHEW 12:36–37

"Do not fear those who kill the body but cannot kill the soul; rather, fear Him who can destroy both soul and body in hell."—MATTHEW 10:28; LUKE 12:4–5

"So it will be at the end of the age. The angels will come out and separate the evil from the righteous and throw them into the furnace of fire, where there will be weeping and gnashing of teeth."—MATTHEW 13:49–50

". . . this generation will be held responsible for the blood of all the prophets that has been shed since the beginning of the world. . . ."—LUKE 11:50

". . . unless you repent, you will all perish. . . ."—LUKE 13:5

BEST-FORGOTTEN TEACHINGS

". . . anyone who divorces his wife, except on the ground of unchastity, causes her to commit adultery; and whoever marries a divorced woman commits adultery."—MATTHEW 5:32; 19:9; MARK 10:11–12; LUKE 16:18

"If your right eye causes you to sin, gouge it out and throw it away. . . . And if your right hand causes you to sin, cut it off and throw it away. It is better for you to lose one part of your body than for your whole body to go into hell."—MATTHEW 5:29–30; 18:8–9; MARK 9:43–47

Many people are familiar with the saying, "Don't throw your pearls before swine." Few are aware of Jesus' conclusion to it. "If you do, they may trample them under their feet, and then turn and tear you to pieces."—MATTHEW 7:6

As to why anyone would *want* to throw pearls in front of pigs, the answer is that Jesus is speaking figuratively. Since he's talking to his disciples, the "pearls" are probably pearls of wisdom, that is, Jesus' teachings. The pigs are never identified.

With his parable of the midnight loaves, Jesus teaches that it's okay to be pushy and annoying as long as the result is worthwhile.—LUKE 11:5–10

With his parable of the rich fool, Jesus teaches that, ". . . those who store up treasures for themselves but are not rich toward God" will be killed—and at the most inopportune moment. —LUKE 12:16–21

With his parable of the wedding feast, Jesus teaches his fellow dinner guests (eat, eat, tubby Jesus) the shrewd, strategic device of lowering expectations to raise one's eventual gain. —LUKE 14:7–11

Jesus tells Peter that he should forgive a brother who sins against him not once, but "seventy times seven." This is odd, since in the verses immediately preceding this teaching Jesus tells his disciples that, "If your brother sins against you . . . and if he refuses to listen even to the church, treat him as you would a pagan or a tax collector."—MATTHEW 18:15–17, 21–22

The parable of the dishonest manager is one that isn't often heard from a pulpit. In it, a manager of a rich man's property is about to be fired for incompetence. But before he can be sacked, the manager goes to all the people who are in debt to the rich man and tells them that it's okay to pay back less than what they owe. When he loses his job, he rationalizes, people will welcome him into their homes.

Does the dishonest manager get socked with divine retribution? Nope. In fact, not only does his plan work perfectly, but the rich man commends him "because he had acted shrewdly." Jesus' moral: ". . . make friends for yourself by means of dishonest wealth so that when it is gone, they may welcome you into the eternal homes."—LUKE 16:1–9

With his parable of the beggar Lazarus and the rich man, Jesus teaches who should go to hell: rich people. After the rich man is sent to Hades, long-dead Abraham explains the dogma that put him there: ". . . remember that in your lifetime you received your good things, while Lazarus received bad things; but now he is comforted [in heaven] and you are in agony."

The scary thing about this parable is that Lazarus and the rich man are one-dimensional; Jesus offers no insight into their character other than that one is rich and one is poor. His lesson is clear: poverty, regardless of how it is attained, guarantees admittance to heaven, and wealth guarantees damnation.

The rich man never argues that he shouldn't be in hell, but he does ask that a warning be sent to his still-living brothers so that they might change their ways. No dice. "They have Moses and the prophets," Abraham snorts. "Let them listen to them." But Moses and the prophets never said *anything* about earthly wealth being a one-way ticket to the fiery furnace. In fact, God rewarded His favorites—like

Abraham—with earthly riches.—LUKE 16:19–31 (see GEN-ESIS 24:34–35)

If you're single when you die, forget about getting married in heaven; Jesus says it never happens.—MARK 12:25; MATTHEW 22:30; LUKE 20:34–35

The parable of the ten minas (i. e., money) is one of the favorites of greedy Christians because it contains the verse, ". . . to all those who have, more will be given. . . ." Jim Bakker liked to pull this quote out of context to justify his self-indulgent brand of Christianity, though it's obvious in context that it refers to the rewards of faith, not of the rich getting richer.—LUKE 19:12–26; 8:18; MATTHEW 25:14–30

Jesus tells his many followers, ". . . my flesh is real food and my blood is real drink. Whoever eats my flesh and drinks my blood remains in me, and I in him." After this discourse, all of his followers desert him except for the twelve disciples.—JOHN 6:53–66

Jesus tells "the Jews" that "you do not belong to my sheep." (JOHN 10:24–26) This passage has been a favorite of Jew-bashers ever since. What the bashers don't mention is that the author of this Gospel, John, often brands all of Jesus' critics as "Jews." Jesus is damning the religious leaders of Jerusalem in John 10, not the Jewish people. Jesus, by the way, was a Jew.

According to Jesus himself, it's the Gentiles, not the Jews, who are the "Christ killers." ". . . The Son of Man will be handed over . . . to the Gentiles," he tells his disciples as he foretells his fate. "They will mock him, and spit upon him, and flog him, and kill him. . . ."—MARK 10:33–34; LUKE 18:32

Part Three: Out with a Wimper

Jesus is told to flee for his life because Herod wants to kill him. Unfortunately, megalomania has set in, robbing Jesus of his earlier good sense: "...I must keep going today and tomorrow and the next day—for surely no prophet can die outside Jerusalem!"—LUKE 13:31–33

*"Oh, God, get this over with." Jesus reluctantly endures
the infamous smooch of a reptilian Judas.*

Jesus, suddenly not quite so cocky as he has been, begs God not to kill him. God doesn't listen.—MATTHEW 26:39–44; MARK 14:32–36; LUKE 22:39–44

The Gospels say that Judas betrayed Jesus with a kiss in front of the crowd that came to arrest him. But why was that necessary? The Gospels repeatedly portray Jesus as well known and immensely popular (MATTHEW 21:8–11), and among the crowd that arrests him are the priests and elders that Jesus had been debating all week at the temple (LUKE 22:52–53). How did he suddenly become so unrecognizable that Judas had to single him out? Couldn't they just look for the guy with the glow around his head?—MATTHEW 26:47–49; MARK 14:43–50; LUKE 22:47–53

Jesus never doubts for a moment that he is the Son of God. He knows, however, should he ever admit it, his enemies will have the proof that they need to have him killed. So Jesus becomes a quick-witted master of evasion, careful never to say what he believes in his heart. But he has no problem when others say it for him.—MATTHEW 16:15–17, 20; MARK 8:27–30; LUKE 9:18–21

What dooms Jesus is that he finally runs out of parables and arcane scripture references to hide behind. Or maybe he just gets tired of the game. When the high priest Caiaphas asks him, "Are you the Messiah, the Son of the Blessed One?" all Jesus can muster is a weak, "I am." The next day he's hanging on the cross.—MARK 14:61–62; MATTHEW 26:63–64; LUKE 22:70

Pontius Pilate, the Roman governor of Judea, is not the villain of Jesus' death, despite his nasty portrayal in wide-screen Hollywood movies. The real scoundrels are the chief priests of the Jerusalem temple, led by Caiaphas.—MATTHEW

27:11–26; Mark 15:1–15; Luke 23:1–23; John 18:28–40; 19:1–16

A young woman named Veronica wipes Jesus' face with her veil after he stumbles carrying the cross, and because his face is saturated with blood, it leaves a mirror-image reproduction on it. The Roman Catholic church eventually made Veronica a saint for her act of pious pity and the Veil of the Holy Face became a treasured relic in Rome. Unfortunately, the Bible makes no mention of any such incident, and in all of its pages, both Old and New Testament, never mentions a single woman named Veronica.

Jesus wasn't killed because of his "radical" teachings. He was killed because the people who attended his trial preferred to set free Barabbas, a much more charismatic radical.—Luke 23:18–21

Some misconceptions about the crucifixion:

Jesus never carried his own cross; some poor guy named Simon was forced—he didn't volunteer—to do it.—Matthew 27:32; Mark 15:21; Luke 23:26

The "Robe" didn't belong to Jesus; it belonged to his guards who made him wear it in the jailhouse but who then took it back before he left.—Matthew 27:31; Mark 15:20

Jesus was fully clothed when he walked to his crucifixion.—Matthew 27:31; Mark 15:20; Luke 23:34

Matthew and Mark mention nothing about Jesus being nailed to his cross. Luke (in the book of Acts) and John do, but only after the fact—they don't mention it until long after Jesus had been dead and buried (and resurrected). And they only mention his hands, not feet.—John 20:25; Acts 2:23

Jesus was mocked, not mourned, by those who passed by.—Matthew 27:39; Mark 15:29

He was also mocked by both of the robbers who were crucified with him.—MATTHEW 27:44; MARK 15:32

Jesus wasn't offered a sponge soaked in vinegar out of nastiness. It was *wine* vinegar in the sponge, and in the context of Matthew and John's Gospel, it was offered as an act of compassion.—MATTHEW 27:48; JOHN 28–30

Jesus' mom didn't attend.—MATTHEW 27:55–56; MARK 15:40

Jesus wasn't jabbed in the side with a spear as an additional torture. He was already dead.—JOHN 19:34

The Gospel according to John disagrees on nearly all of the above points. Because John's version of the crucifixion has the most drama, his is the Gospel that Christians (and Hollywood filmmakers) favor over Matthew, Mark, and Luke. This is a marriage of convenience, however, since John's Gospel fails to include any mention of the Last Supper, the kiss of Judas, the beheading of John the Baptist, Jesus walking on water, or Jesus being born of a virgin and lying in a manger.

One would think that the Gospels would at least agree on Jesus' last recorded words, but they don't:

"My God, my God, why have You forsaken me?"—MATTHEW 27:46; MARK 15:34

"Father, into Your hands I commend my spirit."—LUKE 23:46

"It is finished."—JOHN 19:30

Catholic dogma notwithstanding, the only mention of blood in the crucifixion is in John's brief description of the spear thrust. Jesus never mentions "blood" or "sacrifice" when he tells his disciples about his fate—and he tells them ten times.—MATTHEW 16:21; 17:22–23; 20:17–19; 26:1–2; MARK 8:31; 9:31; 10:33–34; LUKE 9:22, 44; 18:31–33

Jesus' death triggers an invasion of Jerusalem by zombies. "The tombs broke open and the bodies of many holy people who had died were raised to life. They came out of the tombs, and after Jesus' resurrection they went into the holy city and appeared to many people."—MATTHEW 27:52–53

 Dead Jesus fills his disciples with the Holy Ghost by breathing on them.—JOHN 20:22

Even after Jesus is dead, he's hungry. The first time he appears to the disciples after the crucifixion he asks them, "Have you anything here to eat?"—LUKE 24:41

The resurrection seems somewhat less miraculous when
you see that Jesus was buried with a shovel.

Why Did Jesus Fail?

He wanted too much, too soon. Ethical perfection, selfless-ness, and universal, mutual love among all humankind are beautiful, noble goals, but they require at least a twelve-step program to reach them. Jesus didn't want to hear that. There was no, "so far, so good," or "keep going; you're doing great!" in Jesus' lexicon. His agenda was hard and fast and intractable.

One could argue that, in a sense, your curiosity about Jesus after some two thousand years proves that he *didn't* fail. But that's just the kind of conditional, feeble compliment that Jesus would probably hate.

The Disharmony of the Gospels

The Gospels, which all supposedly record the same life of the same man, don't.

Matthew tries to prove that nearly every event in Jesus' life was foretold in the Old Testament and thus that Jesus was the Messiah. To accomplish this, he peppers his Gospel with Old Testament excerpts that are so arcane that they could mean just about anything. Occasionally he'll field one that seems beyond reproach—until one looks up the source and discovers that, in context, it was obviously written about someone other than Jesus (such as Psalm 78:2). Worse still, Matthew deliber-ately alters some of the scriptures that he cites—changing a word here, capitalizing a letter there—to make them prove his point.

Matthew opens his Gospel by listing the "fourteen genera-tions" from the last king of Judah to Joseph, the earthly father of Jesus. He doesn't bolster his credibility as a historian by listing only thirteen names.—MATTHEW 1:12–16

Matthew cites Isaiah's "Immanuel" prophecy (ISAIAH 7:14–17) as proof that Jesus is the Messiah—even though Isaiah didn't claim that Immanuel would *be* a Messiah. Matthew ignores that and boosts his claim by chicanery, changing Isaiah's words from ". . . and [his mother] will call him Immanuel" to ". . . and *they* will call him Immanuel," which leaves open the possibility that Immanuel's name could actually be something else. Like Jesus.—MATTHEW 1:22–23

 It's not recorded anywhere in the Bible, not even in Matthew, that anyone ever called Jesus "Immanuel."

 Matthew's worst corruption of the Old Testament occurs when he claims that the thirty pieces of silver paid to Judas were predicted in the writings of Jeremiah. Jeremiah wrote nothing of the sort; Zechariah was the one who happened to mention thirty pieces of silver. (ZECHARIAH 11:12–13) Matthew apparently remembered the passage but couldn't remember who wrote it.—MATTHEW 27:9–10

Mark presents a more straightforward Gospel than Matthew—as straightforward as a story of a man who raises people from the dead can be. Mark has absolutely nothing to say about Jesus' highly questionable early years (a point in his favor over Matthew and Luke), and his narrative is uncluttered with clumsy attempts to link it to Old Testament prophecies.

Mark also is less in-your-face with his Jesus boosterism than Matthew:

MATTHEW: "Jesus went throughout Galilee . . . curing every disease and every sickness among the people." (4:23)
MARK: ". . . he cured many who were sick with various diseases." (1:34)

MATTHEW: "... Jesus summoned his twelve disciples and gave them authority ... to cure every disease and every sickness ... raise the dead, cleanse the lepers, cast out demons." (10:1, 7)
MARK: "... he appointed twelve ... to be sent out to proclaim the message and to have authority to cast out demons." (3:14–15)

Jesus: "Whoever is not with me is against me...."—MATTHEW 12:30
Jesus: "Whoever is not against us is for us."—MARK 9:40

John's account of Jesus' life differs radically from the three other Gospels, almost as if he were describing another Jesus. The folksy, plain-language parables are gone, and in their place are dense discourses in philosophy, full of mystic imagery. "The wind blows where it chooses, and you hear the sound of it, but you do not know where it comes from or where it goes. So it is with everyone who is born of the Spirit." Jesus is also portrayed as a bit of a prick.

It's very strange that John's Gospel veers so sharply from Matthew's, considering that John and Matthew were supposedly both disciples of the same man. John's Jesus, for example, is unconcerned with proving that events in his life were foretold by Old Testament scriptures. In fact, the Jesus of John makes a number of claims that indicate that he's never read the Old Testament at all:

"No one has ever seen God...." (JOHN 1:18)
Don't tell that to Ezekiel. (EZEKIEL 8:1–2)

"No one has ascended into heaven...." (JOHN 3:13)
Then where did Elijah go? (II KINGS 2:11)

"...God so loved the world that he gave his only son...."
(JOHN 3:16)
Then who were the other "sons of God"? (GENESIS 6:4)

"The Father judges no one...." (JOHN 5:22)
Tell that to all the people He's killed. (PSALM 110:6)

 What's more, John is the only Gospel writer with the nerve to cite a passage from his own book as a scripture reference (JOHN 18:9 cites JOHN 6:39). And he cites it incorrectly.

THE UNGODLY JESUS OF JOHN
The Jesus of John has a snide smugness about him, more akin to a haughty king than a humble healer:

 "I do not accept praise from men...."—JOHN 5:41

"If you believed Moses, you would believe me, for he wrote about me."—JOHN 5:46

 "...I know that his [John the Baptist's] testimony about me is valid.... Not that I accept human testimony; but I mention it that you may be saved."—JOHN 5:32, 34

Jesus reaches his arrogant apex in John's eighth chapter. The Gospel places him in Jerusalem's temple, where he begins lecturing a crowd with the swellheaded boast, "I am the light of the world." He doesn't let up for the next forty-seven verses.

This Jesus is nothing like the "good news" Jesus of Christian coloring books, the grinning guy in the white robe and sandals who cuddles a rainbow coalition of children in his lap. This is a whiny, overbearing know-it-all who can't seem to stop making brazen claims of divine origin.

Some examples of his high-handed circular logic:

"I pass judgment on no one. But if I do judge, my decisions are right...." (JOHN 8:15–16)

"If God were your father, you would love me, for I came from God and now I am here." (JOHN 8:42)

"He who belongs to God hears what God says. The reason you do not hear is that you do not belong to God." (JOHN 8:47)

"... you do not know [God]. But I know Him. If I would say that I do not know Him, I would be a liar like you." (JOHN 8:55)

"If I am telling the truth, why don't you believe me?" (JOHN 8:46)

The people in the temple dismiss Jesus as demon-possessed, and in light of what he's saying, that's understandable. But Jesus doesn't stop. He ends his tirade by proclaiming that, "... before Abraham was, I am!"—a clever (if ungrammatical) reference to Exodus 3:14, in which God tells Moses that *His* name is I Am. The patient people of Jerusalem have had enough: they might tolerate a Jesus who claimed to be a prophet, they might even tolerate a Jesus who claimed to be a Messiah, but to hear Jesus claim that he is God Himself is heresy. They pick up stones and are ready to kill him, but Jesus beats a hasty retreat out of the city.

Jesus utters another indiscreet bombshell: "The Father and I are one." Once again Jesus' audience picks up stones to kill him, once again Jesus runs away.—JOHN 10:30–40

To his credit, John's Jesus does assume a kinder, gentler nature by the end of John's Gospel. In fact, his final speech

to his disciples contains one of the nicest passages attributed
to Jesus anywhere in the Bible: "I give you a new commandment, that you love one another." Nevertheless, he also man-
ages to fire off the following:

 "If you love me, you will obey what I command."—JOHN
14:15

 "If the world hates you, keep in mind that it hated me first."
—JOHN 15:18

Jesus HANGOVER

ith the conclusion of the four Gospels, Jesus disappears from the scene. Unfortunately, so do his teachings. The remaining books of the New Testament (with the exception of Revelation) document what rose in their place: a cult of personality that its followers called, at first, "the Way."

Whereas the first four books of the New Testament chronicled the activities of Jesus, the book of **Acts** chronicles the activities of the apostles, which is what the disciples called themselves after Jesus died (an apostle is a combination evangelist-missionary). These men, lacking the ability to create new teachings, instead fell back on the tactics of Matthew, citing (usually incorrectly) marginal and often altered Old Testament scriptures to prove that Jesus was the Messiah. Instead of crusading for an ethical revolution, they exhorted their followers to repent and be baptized in Jesus' name. (Note: There's no record, anywhere in the Bible, that

Jesus ever baptized anyone.) The apostles had discovered a core tenet of Christianity: that it's easier to worship Jesus than to obey his teachings.

The followers of the Way gradually began to call themselves Christians to honor their dead leader. The idea that God judges everyone alike also gradually changed and a new chosen people with a new set of rituals was born.

Judas, according to the book of Acts, didn't hang himself after he betrayed Jesus (see MATTHEW 27:3–5 for that account). He outlived the Son of Man and bought a field with his thirty pieces of silver. However, God's vengeance wasn't long in coming: Judas exploded in the middle of his field, "and all his bowels gushed out."—ACTS 1:18

The Holy Ghost descends on Jesus' disciples in the form of individual "tongues of fire." They begin to speak the languages of "God-fearing Jews from every nation under heaven," a skill that would obviously help them in their upcoming ministry. Peter tries to explain this strange event to a gathering crowd: "Fellow Jews," he cries. "These men are not drunk, as you suppose."—ACTS 2:1–15

"Now the whole group of those who believed were of one heart and soul, and no one claimed private ownership of any possessions, but everything they owned was held in common." (ACTS 4:32) The life in this early Christian commune may sound idyllic, but it was rough going for those who didn't pay up . . .

". . . A man named Ananias, with the consent of his wife Sapphira, sold a piece of property. With his wife's knowledge he kept back some of the proceeds, and brought only a part and laid it at the apostles' feet. 'Ananias,' Peter asked, 'why has Satan filled your heart to lie to the Holy Spirit and to keep back part of the proceeds for the land? You did not lie to us,

Snazzy balls of flame were a gift to early Christians from God, who apparently didn't realize that Christian stalkers would find them very useful.

but to God!' Now when Ananias heard these words, he fell down and died.

"After an interval of about three hours his wife came in, not knowing what had happened. Peter said to her, 'Tell me whether you and your husband sold the land for such and such a price.' And she said, 'Yes, that was the price.'

"Then Peter said to her, 'How is it that you have agreed together to put the Spirit of the Lord to the test? Look! The feet of those who have buried your husband are at the door, and they will carry you out also.'

"Immediately she fell down at his feet and died."—Acts 5:1–11

The elders of Israel have the apostles flogged for teaching about Jesus. The apostles rejoice at their torture, "because they had been counted worthy of suffering disgrace for the Name." Christian masochism is born.—ACTS 5:41

Stephen, one of the subapostles (not one of the top twelve), has the honor of being the first follower of the Way to be

"Take that, you flame head!" The apostle Stephen gets the Christian religion off to a rocky start.

murdered. He brings it about in a manner reminiscent of John's Jesus: he harangues his accusers for fifty-two verses, ends his discourse with an insult, and then is dragged outside and stoned to death.—ACTS 7

Ananias, also a subapostle, is the first person in the Bible to refer to apostles as "saints"—a notion that the Catholic church would promote vigorously in the years to come.—ACTS 9:13

The Good News Bible, no fan of Catholicism, has expunged all 101 "saint" references from its pages.

Peter is ordered by God to bring the Gospel of Jesus to the Gentiles. The order comes in a surreal vision of a huge sheet filled with animals, floating down from heaven, over which God repeatedly commands, "Kill and eat."—ACTS 10:9–28

First appearance in the Bible of the word *Christian*.—ACTS 11:26

God finally kills evil King Herod, not for all the human suffering he's caused but because his followers tell him he has "the voice of a god" and Herod doesn't dispute it. "Immediately . . . an angel of the Lord struck him down, and he was eaten by worms and died."—ACTS 12:21–23

The apostle Paul engages in metaphysical battle with an evil sorcerer named Bar-Jesus on the island of Cyprus. "You are a child of the Devil," Paul cries, "and an enemy of everything that is right!" God blinds Bar-Jesus.—ACTS 13:6–11

SAUL OF TARSUS

As far as Christianity is concerned, the most important person in the New Testament is not Jesus. Nor is it Peter, the

"Vicar of Christ," who led the disciples in the first years after Jesus' death. It is instead Saul of Tarsus, an apostle-come-lately who had never even met Jesus.

Saul (who later renamed himself the apostle Paul) was the first Christian missionary, a classic type-A overachiever possessed of too much energy and not enough comprehension. He rapidly rose to the top of the apostle heap, bypassing even Peter—the Jesus-proclaimed "rock" of the ministry—as his Gentile-based church in Antioch bypassed the Jew-based church in Jerusalem. The result of Paul's Herculean efforts are twofold: 1) Jesus has become one of the best-known men in world history, and 2) Jesus' teachings have been ripped to pieces.

Paul understood that in order for this new religion to flourish it needed to be appealing to both Gentiles and Jews, and to do that he replaced Jesus' message with metaphysical doctrine, something more difficult to grasp but infinitely easier to live with. His businesslike mind could not conceive of Jesus' selfless, love-based anarchy, so he replaced that with a church hierarchy, a series of home offices, and a multitude of rules. Paul organized Christianity to make it successful, and Christianity had to be successful because Paul had to be successful. He couldn't bear the thought of dying as an unheralded martyr, like Jesus.

Without Paul, the Way would probably have remained an insignificant Jewish sect, dead and long forgotten. With him—his fanatic energy, his political savvy in baptizing Gentiles whenever Jews balked, and his genius for ignoring the substance of Jesus' teachings—it became Catholicism, the most powerful church that the world has ever known.

First book burning in the name of Jesus.—ACTS 19:17–19

Paul talks so long in the city of Troas that one of his listeners falls asleep and then falls out of a third-floor window and dies.

Paul, mindful that this awkward incident might overshadow his talk, rushes downstairs, brings the listener back to life (no credit given to God), and then continues talking until daylight.—ACTS 20:7–12

In Paul's final speech to the church leaders at Ephesus he proclaims, "...we must support the weak, remembering the words of the Lord Jesus, for he himself said: 'It is more blessed to give than to receive.'" That sounds nice, but the Bible doesn't record that Jesus ever said any such thing.—ACTS 20:35

Though the epistle writers often follow the example of Matthew and quote Old Testament scripture by the scrollful, they only twice cite incidents that appear in the Gospels: the Last Supper (I CORINTHIANS 11:23–25) and the Transfiguration (II PETER 1:17–18). These writers, many of whom supposedly knew Jesus intimately, make no mention of his miraculous birth, his many outstanding miracles, or even of the more dramatic details of his death. These are extraordinary omissions, considering that the epistle writers otherwise try so hard to convince their readers that Jesus was the Son of God.

One could conclude from this that the Gospels, supposedly contemporary accounts of the events that surrounded Jesus' life, were actually works of fiction written long, long after his death—even after most of the epistles. And one could be right.

Paul returns to Jerusalem to preach at its temple, but the Jews of Judea aren't buying his monkey-business mixing of Jews and Gentiles. "Rid the earth of him!" they howl. "He's not fit to live!" Paul is nearly killed, and this nasty reception makes clear what the Bible never says outright: that Paul is preaching a very different form of Christianity from the Jewish apostles in Jerusalem.—ACTS 21:20–22, 27–36; 22:21–29

 Festus, the Roman governor of Judea, provides a rare outsider's view of a Bible story when he explains Paul's temple confrontation to King Agrippa: "When his accusers got up to speak," Festus tells the king, "they did not charge him with any of the crimes I had expected. Instead, they had some points of dispute with him about their own religion and about a dead man named Jesus who Paul claimed was alive."—ACTS 25:18–19

 Only mention in the Bible of lesbianism: ". . . God gave [the idol worshippers] over to shameful lusts. Even their women exchanged natural relations for unnatural ones."—ROMANS 1:26–27

THE EPISTLES

After the book of Acts come the "epistles," twenty-one letters written by the apostles in the very early years of the Christian church. The epistles are all talk and no action, and although they offer invaluable glimpses of the slow corruption of Jesus' teachings, they also make for grueling reading.

Busy-beaver Paul wrote the first thirteen of the epistles: **Romans, I** and **II Corinthians, Galatians, Ephesians, Philippians, Colossians, I** and **II Thessalonians, I** and **II Timothy, Titus,** and **Philemon.** These serve as Paul's soapbox for delivering his interpretations of Christian doctrine.

Paul tries very hard to "explain" Jesus; to make following him a rational exercise; to make his message acceptable to Gentiles while still complying with Jewish religious dogma. To accomplish this he performs a theological miracle, transforming Jesus' moral rebellion into an organized religion.

Paul's Unique Interpretation of God and Jesus

Early Christian philosophy is so tenuous and full of metaphysical mumbo jumbo that even the various Bible translations often disagree on exactly what's being said. The excerpts that follow are, as throughout this book, based on the New Revised Standard and New International Bibles, but if the words in your Bible vary significantly, don't be surprised.

". . . if you confess with your lips that Jesus is Lord and believe in your heart that God raised him from the dead, you will be saved."—ROMANS 10:9

". . . we are always being given up to death for Jesus' sake, so that the life of Jesus may be made visible in our mortal flesh."—II CORINTHIANS 4:11

". . . the Scripture declares that the whole world is a prisoner of sin. . . ."—GALATIANS 3:22

". . . through [the Jews'] stumbling, salvation has come to the Gentiles, so as to make Israel jealous."—ROMANS 11:11

Paul is adept at changing Jesus' straightforward and understandable teachings into abstract and shamelessly forced allegories: "In [Jesus] you were . . . circumcised, in the putting off of the sinful nature, not with a circumcision done by the hands of men but with the circumcision done by Christ, having been buried with him in baptism and raised with him through your faith in the power of God, who raised him from the dead. He forgave us all our sins, having canceled the written code, with its regulations, that was against us and stood opposed to us; he took it away, nailing it to the cross."
—COLOSSIANS 2:11–14

Paul explains that God specifically chooses poor and stupid people to be Christians so that He'll seem more powerful when the Christians triumph over rich and smart people. —I Corinthians 1:26–29

Christians Are Above the Law

 "... a person is justified not by the works of the law, but through faith in Jesus Christ."—Galatians 2:16

 "... if justification comes through the law, then Christ died for nothing."—Galatians 2:21

 "Now that faith has come, we are no longer under the supervision of the law."—Galatians 3:25

 Paul splits many scriptural hairs in an effort to validate his argument that faith overrules Judaic law. He insists that the covenant made between God and Abraham and his "offspring" has been misinterpreted; the offspring is Jesus, not the Jews, otherwise the scripture would've read "offsprings." He declares that the "promise" made by God to Abraham existed before the "law." ("If you belong to Christ, then you are Abraham's offspring and heirs according to the promise.") But, honestly, who really cares? Jesus never said anything about any of this stuff, but Paul never concerns himself with Jesus' teachings; his goal is to get Gentiles into the church, and the only way that he can justify such radical action is with his faith-trumps-law argument.—Galatians 3:10–20, 29

A New Chosen People

 "... it is not the natural children [the Jews] who are God's children, but it is the children of the promise [the Christians] who are regarded as Abraham's offspring."—Romans 9:8

Paul woos the Gentiles by comparing the welcoming Christian church to the exclusionary Jewish faith: "... remember ... you were separate from Christ, excluded from citizenship in Israel, and foreigners to the covenants of promise, without hope and without God in the world. But now in Christ Jesus you who were far away have been brought near...."—EPHESIANS 2:12–13

"... [the Jews] killed both the Lord Jesus and the prophets and drove us out; they displease God and oppose everyone by hindering us from speaking to Gentiles so that they may be saved."—I THESSALONIANS 2:15–16

Paul has harsh words for those who insist that Christians must subscribe to Judaic law. He calls them "... dogs ... evil workers ... those who mutilate the flesh! For it is we who are the circumcision...."—PHILIPPIANS 3:2–3

"... there are many rebellious people, mere talkers and deceivers, especially those of the circumcision group. They must be silenced ... pay no attention to Jewish myths ... both their minds and consciences are corrupted. They claim to know God, but by their actions they deny him. They are detestable, disobedient, and unfit for doing anything good."— TITUS 1:10–16

Cynical Paul
"To the Jews I became as a Jew, in order to win Jews. To those under the law I became as one under the law (though I myself am not under the law) so that I might win those under the law.... To the weak I became weak, so that I might win the weak. I have become all things to all people, that I might by all means save some. I do it all for the sake of the gospel, so that I may share in its blessings."—I CORINTHIANS 9:20–23

Paul doesn't mind if the Gospel of Jesus is preached out of "envy" or "selfish ambition." ". . . What does it matter?" he writes to the church at Philippia. "The important thing is that in every way, whether from false motives or true, Christ is preached."—PHILIPPIANS 1:15–18

"Teach slaves to be subject to their masters in everything, to try to please them, not to talk back to them . . . so that in every way they will make the teaching about God our Savior attractive."—TITUS 2:9–10

Christians Need Money More Than Jesus

Paul wants the Corinthians to increase their "grace of giving" by donating more money to the church. To achieve this, he heaps guilt on their heads by lauding the generosity of the church of Macedonia. "I am not commanding you," Paul writes in his greasiest prose, "but I want to test the sincerity of your love by comparing it with the earnestness of others."
—II CORINTHIANS 8:1–15

Next, Paul plays his threat-of-humiliation card: ". . . I know your eagerness to help, and I have been boasting about it to the Macedonians, telling them that since last year you . . . were ready to give; and your enthusiasm has stirred most of them to action. But I am sending [personal representatives] in order that our boasting about you in this matter should not prove hollow, but that you may be ready, as I said you would be. For if any Macedonians come with me and find you unprepared we—not to say anything about you—would be ashamed of having been so confident."—II CORINTHIANS 9:2–4

"God loves a cheerful giver."—II CORINTHIANS 9:7

Paul: An Ego of Biblical Proportions

"It has always been my ambition to preach the gospel where Christ was not known, so that I would not be building on someone else's foundation."—ROMANS 15:20

"Do everything without complaining or arguing . . . in order that I may boast on the day of Christ that I did not run or labor for nothing."—PHILIPPIANS 2:14–16

"Do you not know that in a race all the runners run, but only one gets the prize? . . . I beat my body and make it my slave so that after I have preached to others, I myself will not be disqualified for the prize."—I CORINTHIANS 9:24–27

"I have fought the good fight, I have finished the race, I have kept the faith. From now on there is reserved for me the crown of righteousness, which the Lord, the righteous Judge, will give me. . . ."—II TIMOTHY 4:7–8

Paul tells the Galatian church that he wishes that Christians who spread teachings other than his would cut off their penises.—GALATIANS 5:12

The Hell of Not Being Sure

". . . if Christ has not been raised, our preaching is useless and so is your faith."—I CORINTHIANS 15:14

"If only for this life we have hope in Christ, we are to be pitied more than all men."—I CORINTHIANS 15:19

The Downside of Being Saved

". . . you have been freed from sin and enslaved to God. . . ."
—ROMANS 6:22

"You are not your own; you were bought at a price."—I Corinthians 6:19–20

"Shun fornication! All other sins that a person commits are outside his body, but the fornicator sins against the body itself. Or do you not know that your body is a temple of the Holy Spirit within you, which you have from God, and that you are not your own?"—I Corinthians 6:18–19

"Do you not know that your bodies are members of Christ himself? Shall I then take the members of Christ and unite them with a prostitute? Never!"—I Corinthians 6:15

Paul Loathes the Ladies

"If a woman does not cover her head, she should have her hair cut off.... A man ought not to cover his head, since he is the image and glory of God; but the woman is the glory of man. For this reason, and because of the angels, the woman ought to have a sign of authority over her head.

"Does not the very nature of things teach you that if a man has long hair it is a disgrace to him, but that if a woman has long hair it is her glory? For long hair is given to her as a covering."—I Corinthians 11:3–15

"... women should be silent in the churches. For they are not permitted to speak, but should be subordinate, as the law also says. If there is anything they desire to know, let them ask their husbands at home...."—I Corinthians 14:34–35

"Wives, submit to your husbands as to the Lord. For the husband is the head of the wife as Christ is the head of the church ... as the church submits to Christ, so also wives should submit to their husbands in everything."—Ephesians 5:22–24

"I . . . want women to dress modestly, with decency and propriety, not with braided hair or gold or jewels or expensive clothes. . . . A woman should learn in quietness and full submission. I do not permit a woman to teach or to have authority over a man; she must be silent. For Adam was formed first, then Eve. And Adam was not the one deceived; it was the woman who was deceived and became a sinner. But women will be saved through childbearing. . . ."—I TIMOTHY 2:9–14

"No widow may be put on the list [of those to be helped] unless she is over sixty, has been faithful to her husband, and is well known for her good deeds, such as bringing up children, showing hospitality, washing the feet of the saints. . . .

"As for younger widows, do not put them on the list. For when their sensual desires overcome their dedication to Christ, they want to marry. . . . Besides, they get into the habit of being idle . . . gossips and busybodies. . . ."—I TIMOTHY 5:9–13

Marriage Counselor Paul

"It is good for a man not to marry. But since there is so much immorality, each man should have his own wife, and each woman her own husband."—I CORINTHIANS 7:1–2

"Do not deprive one another except perhaps by agreement for a set time to devote yourselves to prayer, and then come together again, so that Satan may not tempt you because of your lack of self-control."—I CORINTHIANS 7:5

"If anyone . . . feels he ought to marry, he should do as he wants . . . but he who does not marry . . . does even better." —I CORINTHIANS 7:36–38

Know Your Place

"...who are you, O man, to talk back to God? Does not the potter have the right to make out of the same lump of clay some pottery for noble purposes and some for common use?"—ROMANS 9:20–21

 "The authorities that exist have been established by God. Consequently, he who rebels against the authority is rebelling against what God has instituted, and those who do so will bring judgment on themselves."—ROMANS 13:1–2

 "Slaves, obey your earthly masters with respect and fear, and with sincerity of heart, just as you would obey Christ. Obey them not only to win their favor when their eye is on you, but like slaves of Christ, doing the will of God from your heart. Serve wholeheartedly, as if you were serving the Lord...."
—EPHESIANS 6:5–7

The REALLY Weird Beliefs of Paul

 "Do you not know that all of us who have been baptized into Christ Jesus were baptized into his death? Therefore we have been buried with him by baptism into death...."—ROMANS 6:3–4

 "...[God] has graciously granted you the privilege not only of believing in Christ, but of suffering for him as well...."
—PHILIPPIANS 1:29

 "...if I do what I do not want, it is no longer I that do it, but sin that dwells within me."—ROMANS 7:20

 "If we are out of our mind, it is for the sake of God...."
—II CORINTHIANS 5:13

"...everything that does not come from faith is sin." —ROMANS 14:23

"We know that Christ, being raised from the dead, will never die again...."—ROMANS 6:9

"...through the law I died to the law so that I might live to God. I have been crucified with Christ and it is no longer I who live, but it is Christ who lives in me."—GALATIANS 2:19–20

"Whoever...eats the bread or drinks the cup of the Lord in an unworthy manner will be answerable for the body and blood of the Lord. For this reason many of you are weak and ill, and some have died."—I CORINTHIANS 11:27–30

"...we are to God the aroma of Christ among those who are being saved and those who are perishing. To the one we are the smell of death; to the other, the fragrance of life." —II CORINTHIANS 2:15–16

"Godly sorrow brings repentance that leads to salvation and leaves no regret, but worldly sorrow brings death."—II CORINTHIANS 7:10

"...In order that sin might be recognized as sin, it produced death in me through what was good, so that through the commandment sin might become utterly sinful."—ROMANS 7:13

It's also Paul who comes up with the systematic, unimaginably tedious idea that everyone who dies will have to stand trial before God: "...we will all stand before God's judgment seat...each of us will give an account of himself to God." —ROMANS 14:10, 12

...And a Rare Moment of Pseudosanity

"I thank God that I speak in tongues more than all of you; nevertheless, in church I would rather speak five words with my mind, in order to instruct others, than ten thousand words in a tongue.... If the whole church comes together and all speak in tongues, and outsiders or unbelievers enter, will they not say that you are out of your mind?"—I CORINTHIANS 14:18–19, 23

After the epistles of Paul there are eight more, penned by various Christian apostles in the very early years of the church. These are **Hebrews, James, I** and **II Peter, I, II,** and **III John,** and **Jude.**

The epistle of **Hebrews** tries harder than any other to link Jesus to Judaism's grisly, heavy-handed religious dogma. It repeatedly refers to Jesus as "the high priest" and uses Old Testament orthodoxy to wedge the new Christian hoodoo into the old Hebrew mold. The arguments put forth in Hebrews may be forced, but they make no less sense than the pro-Gentile rantings of Paul.

"...the first covenant had regulations for worship and also an earthly sanctuary. A tabernacle was set up. But only the high priest entered the inner room, and that only once a year, and never without blood....

"When Christ came as the high priest...he went through the greater and more perfect tabernacle that is not man-made.... He did not enter by means of the blood of goats and calves; but he entered the Most Holy Place once and for all by his own blood...."—HEBREWS 9:1–2, 7, 11–12

"...without the shedding of blood there is no forgiveness of sins."—HEBREWS 9:22

"Anyone who has violated the law of Moses dies without mercy 'on the testimony of two or three witnesses.' How much worse punishment do you think will be deserved by those who have spurned the Son of God?... It is a fearful thing to fall into the hands of the living God."—HEBREWS 10:28–31

"... the Lord disciplines those He loves, and He punishes everyone He accepts as a son."—HEBREWS 12:6

The epistle of **James** may have been written by Jesus' brother, which helps to explain how this generally undistinguished letter got into the New Testament.

"If any of you lacks wisdom, he should ask God.... But when he asks, he must believe and not doubt, because he who doubts ... is a double-minded man, unstable in all he does."—JAMES 1:5–8

"The tongue is ... a fire, a world of evil among the parts of the body. It corrupts the whole person, sets the whole course of his life on fire, and is itself set on fire by hell."—JAMES 3:6

"Whoever wishes to become a friend of the world becomes an enemy of God."—JAMES 4:4

Peter was the #1 disciple while Jesus lived, but he was quickly overshadowed by the apostle Paul after Jesus died. The epistles **I** and **II Peter** are Peter's chance to make himself heard in the Bible. Perhaps he shouldn't have bothered.

"... you ... like living stones, are being built into a spiritual house...."—I PETER 2:5

"... God waited patiently in the days of Noah while the ark

was being built. In it, only a few people... were saved through water, and this water symbolizes baptism that now saves you also...."—I PETER 3:20–21

"...in the last days scoffers will come.... They will say, 'Where is this "coming" He promised? Ever since our fathers died, everything goes on as it did since the beginning of creation.' But do not forget... with the Lord a day is like a thousand years and a thousand years are like a day. The Lord is not slow in keeping His promise.... He is patient... not wanting anyone to perish, but everyone to come to repentance."—II PETER 3:3–4, 8–9

In **I, II,** and **III John** the apostle John sheds his nasty gospel persona and becomes the closest thing in the Bible to a hippie. His first epistle contains the highest density of the word "love" to be found anywhere in the Bible. All is not bliss, however, in John's universe: he mixes his happy hippie talk with an equal share of fear mongering about the antichrist.

"...it is the last hour... [the] antichrist is coming...."—I JOHN 2:18

"...the whole world is under the control of the evil one...."—I JOHN 5:19

First appearance in the Bible of the phrase "God is love." This is on page 907 of a 923-page Bible.—I JOHN 4:8

John's definition of love, "...that we walk in obedience to God's commands," is something that is *not* normally quoted by Jesus hippies.—II JOHN 1:6

John's Circular Logic

John's frequent lapses into circular logic hint that John was relying on something more than faith to attain ecstasy:

"No one who is born of God will continue to sin, because God's seed remains in him; he cannot go on sinning because he has been born of God."—I JOHN 3:9

"Those who do not believe in God have made Him a liar by not believing in the testimony that God has given. . . ."—I JOHN 5:10

"We are from God. Whoever knows God listens to us, and whoever is not from God does not listen to us."—I JOHN 4:6

". . . if we know that [God] hears us—whatever we ask—we know that we have what we asked of Him."—I JOHN 5:15

Jude was another brother of Jesus. This perhaps explains how, in his brief epistle, he is able to casually mention Old Testament incidents that do not appear anywhere in the Old Testament.

VERSE 6: ". . . the angels who did not keep their positions of authority but abandoned their own home—these [God] has kept in darkness, bound with everlasting chains for judgment on the great Day." This is an elaboration of an idea that makes its only other appearance in II Peter 2:4 and sounds suspiciously like "the fall" Milton wrote about in *Paradise Lost*. But where the story came from (and where Milton got all his other details) is missing from the Bible.

VERSE 9: ". . . the archangel Michael, when he was disputing with the Devil about the body of Moses, did not dare to bring a slanderous accusation against him. . . ." Nothing of the sort is mentioned in Deuteronomy 34, which states simply that Moses died and was buried by God in an unmarked grave.

VERSE 14: ". . . Enoch, in the seventh generation from Adam, prophesied, saying, 'See, the Lord is coming with ten thousands of His holy ones to execute judgment on all, and to convict everyone of all the deeds of ungodliness that they have committed. . . .'" The brief description of Enoch in Genesis 5 mentions no such thing. But if it's true, and if Jude's assertion that Enoch lived only seven generations after Adam is correct, then Enoch wins the prize as the most precocious Gloomy Gus in the Bible.

THE TERRIFYING FUTURE

The book of **Revelation** is, hands down, the Bible's most deranged. It was written by the apostle John, and if his epistles can be seen as John on pot, then Revelation is John on acid.

The revelation in Revelation is one that describes the end of the earth ("apocalypse" is Greek for "revelation") and the arrival of the Kingdom of Heaven. John asserts that this revelation was given to him by Jesus, whom he describes as having glowing feet and a sword sticking out of his mouth. This is typical of John's attention to detail. Unlike the apocalypse described by Daniel, which was complicated and murky, John's vision, while complex, is pinpoint specific.

Revelation joins Ecclesiastes and The Song of Songs as the Bible's most oddball books. They've survived because they were supposedly penned by biblical superstars—Solomon and the apostle John—and because the men who codified the Scriptures placed more value on Big Names than on a neat, sanitized Bible.

Revelation is a window into the mind of a maniac. John wasn't just another God-skewed zealot, he was a man who needed to be locked up and put on Librium.

Some Highlights
Philadelphia has the honor of being the only American city named in apocalyptic Bible literature.—REVELATION 3:7

John provides the only biblical description of heaven—a surreal, terrifying place that only a madman could enjoy: "...before me was a throne...and the One who sat there had the appearance of jasper.... From the throne came flashes of lightning, rumblings and peals of thunder.... Around the throne were four living creatures, and they were covered with eyes, in front and in back.... Day and night they never stop saying: 'Holy, holy, holy is the Lord God Almighty, who was, and is, and is to come.'"—REVELATION 4:2–8

John adds that the ark of the covenant is in heaven, a place that certainly seems fitting for it.—REVELATION 11:19

When John says that God looks like jasper, what he's saying is that God is *green*.

John notes that the 144,000 living people who will be deemed worthy of salvation during the final judgment "did not defile themselves with women, for they kept themselves pure." This means that none of the saved will be lesbians or, one could assume, women, period.—REVELATION 14:3–4

Jesus tells John that he is "the Offspring of David and the bright Morning Star," which means that Jesus' mom is actually the planet Venus.—REVELATION 22:16

The preceding translation is from the New International and King James versions of the Bible. The Good News version translates it as, "I am descended from the family of David; I am the bright morning star." This means that Jesus *is* the planet Venus. Take your pick.

THE FINAL JUDGMENT

"Judgment Day" is only the climax of a long series of strange events that constitute the end of the world, aka the Final Judgment. John's description of the Judgment takes up most of the last eighteen chapters in Revelation. Here are the highlights:

Jesus, who in heaven resembles a dead lamb with seven horns and seven eyes (John's attention to detail once again), pulls seals off of a scroll held by God. This activity unleashes a series of calamities on the earth. However, the carnage is temporarily halted while an angel marks the foreheads of the 144,000 people to be saved.

Then the calamities resume: the earth is bombarded with "hail and fire mixed with blood" and many other unpleasant things. The gates of hell are opened and out pour locusts with human faces, wearing tiny crowns, that sting people with their tails for five months. Then two hundred million angels, riding horses with lion heads that breathe sulfur and flame, kill a third of humankind.

Next, a lull. Two prophets appear on the earth, packing a variety of deadly supernatural powers. For 1,260 days they torment humankind. Then they're killed by "the beast" from hell, but after three and a half days they're resurrected and go to heaven. This is announced by an earthquake that kills seven thousand people.

At about this same time war breaks out in heaven; the angel Michael triumphs and hurls the Devil down to earth.

The Devil teams up with a second beast (not the original beast), and they make life miserable for God's chosen people for forty-two months. Then the first beast reappears and forces everyone either to worship the second beast or be killed. The worshippers receive the "mark of the beast." (Christian fundamentalists never mention that the 144,000 God-fearing folk who've survived have also been marked, thus *everyone* has a mark on their forehead.)

God's bloodbath resumes: angels with giant sickles kill thousands, plagues and hailstones pick off the survivors, earthquakes level cities including Babylon, "the great whore." The second beast and the first beast (now renamed "the false prophet") are thrown into a lake of burning sulfur. Every soldier in their vast army is killed in the battle of Armageddon by the sword-wielding mouth of a creature named Word of God. Their flesh is eaten by birds.

An angel grabs the Devil, wraps him in a chain, and throws him into hell. This signals the first resurrection, which only applies to those who have been beheaded because they stuck up for Jesus.

After a thousand years, the Devil is released from hell. He gathers yet another vast army ("Gog and Magog") to do battle, but they're consumed by fire sent down from heaven. Then the Devil is thrown into the same lake of sulfur as the beast and the false prophet.

This signals the second resurrection: Judgment Day, the main event. Everybody is raised from the dead (apparently no humans have survived), paraded before a big, white throne, and anyone whose name isn't written in the book of life is thrown into the lake of sulfur.

Heaven, hell, the earth, and death all disappear. They are replaced by a new earth and a new heaven, from which descends "the new Jerusalem," a city made of pure gold, occupying fifteen hundred cubic miles.

"Hi-ho Pestilence! Awaaay!" The Four Horsemen of the Apocalypse ride into town with their divine wrath blazing.

John, whose descriptions have been painfully detailed up to this point, becomes suspiciously mum when it comes to describing what life is like in the new Jerusalem. He mentions only that it will always be daylight, that its inhabitants will serve God and Jesus, and that no "sexually immoral" people will be allowed in it.

That's it. The end. Of Revelation, of the New Testament, of the Bible.

". . . the time is near," Jesus says in the Bible's final chapter. "I am coming soon!" Two thousand years later, the faithful still wait.

Embarrassing Bible Questions

- ‡ Do you really believe that Noah was five hundred years old when he fathered his first child?—GENESIS 5:32

- ‡ Why was it okay for God to destroy the sinful city of Sodom but not okay to destroy Lot's daughters when they had sex with him?—GENESIS 19:30–36

- ‡ If God is all-powerful, how come He lost His wrestling match with Jacob?—GENESIS 32:24–30

- ‡ Do you really believe that anyone who works on a religious "day of rest" should be killed?—EXODUS 31:15

- ‡ Do you believe in killing children? Then why did God allow Jephthah to sacrifice his virgin daughter?—JUDGES 11:30–39

- ‡ Do you believe that children should be put to death for the sins of their parents? Then why did God kill David and Bathsheba's baby but let David and Bathsheba live? —II SAMUEL 11:2–4, 14–27; 12:9–19

- ‡ If God is all-powerful, how come God's armies were defeated by the king of Moab after the king sacrificed his son to the god Chemosh?—II KINGS 3:18–19, 26–27

- ‡ Do you believe that holiness can be transferred by clothing? God does.—EZEKIEL 44:19

- Do you believe that if your hand or your eye causes you to sin, it should be ripped out of your body? Jesus did. —MATTHEW 5:29–30

- How come God rewarded Abraham and Lot with earthly riches but Jesus said that wealth is a one-way ticket to hell?—GENESIS 24:34–35; JOB 42:10–12; MATTHEW 19:24

- Do you believe in slavery? Then how come no one in the Bible—not even Jesus—criticizes it? How come the apostles Paul and Peter encourage slaves to be obedient? —EPHESIANS 6:5–7; I PETER 2:18

- Do you believe that Jesus is actually the planet Venus? He did.—REVELATION 22:16

- Three times in the final chapter of the Bible, Jesus says "I am coming soon!" That was written almost two thousand years ago. How come he hasn't shown up yet?—REVELATION 22:12–13

Ken's Concordances

BIBLE SEX CONCORDANCE

Adam and Eve—Genesis 4:1
Cain and his unnamed wife—Genesis 4:17
Adam and Eve #2—Genesis 4:25
The sons of God and human women—Genesis 6:2, 4
Sarai and the Pharaoh—Genesis 12:14–19
Abram and Hagar—Genesis 16:4
Two angels and the men of Sodom (unconsummated)—Genesis 19:4–5
Lot and his daughters (forced)—Genesis 19:30–36
Isaac and Rebekah—Genesis 24:67
Jacob and Leah—Genesis 29:23
Jacob and Rachel—Genesis 29:30
Jacob and Bilhah—Genesis 30:4
Jacob and Zilpah—Genesis 30:9–10
Jacob and Leah #2—Genesis 30:16
Shechem and Dinah (forced)—Genesis 34:2
Reuben and Bilhah—Genesis 35:22
Onan and Tamar—Genesis 38:9
Judah and Tamar—Genesis 38:18
Joseph and Potiphar's wife (unconsummated)—Genesis 39:7, 10–12
God's laundry list of sex taboos—Leviticus 18:1–23
Sex taboos punishable by banishment or death—Leviticus 20:10–21
The trial by ordeal for the unfaithful wife—Numbers 5:11–31

The men of Israel and the women of Moab—NUMBERS 25:1
More sex taboos—DEUTERONOMY 22:13–30
Samson and an unnamed prostitute—JUDGES 16:1
The men of Gibeah and an unnamed woman (forced)—JUDGES
    19:25
Boaz and Ruth—RUTH 4:13
Elkanah and Hannah—I SAMUEL 1:19
Eli's sons and the women servants—I SAMUEL 2:22
David and Bathsheba—II SAMUEL 11:4
David and Bathsheba #2—II SAMUEL 12:24
Amnon and Tamar (forced)—II SAMUEL 13:11–14
Ahasuerus/Xerxes and Esther—ESTHER 2:16
The adulteress and the youth who lacked judgment—PROVERBS
    7:6–23
The bride and the bridegroom—SONG OF SONGS (pick any
    verse)
The men of Medes and the wives of Babylon (forced)—ISAIAH
    13:16
The men of Jerusalem and numerous prostitutes—JEREMIAH
    5:7–8
Jerusalem and "anyone who passed by" (an allegory)—EZEKIEL
    16:25–34
The men of Jerusalem: various debaucheries—EZEKIEL 22:10–12
Oholah and Oholibah and the men of many nations (another
    allegory)—EZEKIEL 23:1–21
The women of Judah and unidentified men (forced)—LAMEN-
    TATIONS 5:11
Hosea and Gomer—HOSEA 1:2–3
The people of Israel: various debaucheries—HOSEA 4:13–14
The women of Jerusalem and the men of "all the nations"
    (forced)—ZECHARIAH 14:2
Mary and the Holy Ghost—LUKE 1:35–38
Jesus proclaims that men who marry divorced women commit
    adultery—LUKE 16:18

Homosexual practices among the godless—ROMANS 1:26–27

An unnamed man of Corinth and his (step?)mother—I CORINTHIANS 5:1

The apostle Paul condemns sexual immorality—I CORINTHIANS 6:13–20

The apostle Paul endorses sex within marriage, sort of—I CORINTHIANS 7:1–7

The apostle John notes that those who've had sex with women will not be saved—REVELATION 14:3–4

BONUS ANTI-ABORTIONIST HORROR CONCORDANCE

References to Pregnant Women Being Ripped Open

By the Syrians—II KINGS 8:12

By Menahem, the King of Israel—II KINGS 15:16

By unidentified attackers—HOSEA 13:16†

By the Ammonites—AMOS 1:13

References to Children Being Murdered

Midianite children—NUMBERS 31:17†

Heshbonite children—DEUTERONOMY 2:34†

Bashanite children—DEUTERONOMY 3:6†

Israelite children—II KINGS 8:12

Babylonian children—PSALMS 137:9†

Babylonian children—ISAIAH 13:16†

Beth-Arbelite children—HOSEA 10:14

Israelite children—HOSEA 13:16†

Thebian children—NAHUM 3:10

Bethlehemite children—MATTHEW 2:16

† with God's approval

My Favorite Bible Verses

_____

_____

_____

_____

_____

_____

_____

_____

_____

_____

_____

_____

_____

_____

_____

_____

_____

_____

_____

_____

_____

_____

_____

_____

_____

_____